SEARCHING MESSAGES FROM THE MINOR PROPHETS

Searching Messages from the Minor Prophets

SEARCHING MESSAGES FROM THE MINOR PROPHETS

Volume 1
Joel to Micah

With Introductions and Concise Commentaries

Malcolm C Davis

RITCHIE
John Ritchie Publishing
40 Beansburn, Kilmarnock, Scotland

ISBN-13: 978 1 912522 31 6

Copyright © 2018 by John Ritchie Ltd.
40 Beansburn, Kilmarnock, Scotland

www.ritchiechristianmedia.co.uk

All rights reserved. No part of this publication may be reproduced, stored in a retrievable system, or transmitted in any form or by any other means – electronic, mechanical, photocopy, recording or otherwise – without prior permission of the copyright owner.

Typeset by John Ritchie Ltd., Kilmarnock
Printed by Bell & Bain Ltd., Glasgow

Dedication

To Dr Donald C.B. Cameron, B.Th., M.A., Ph.D., former Army officer and leadership consultant, who has written ten instructive books on Bible prophecy and encouraged me during the writing of mine on similar subjects

Acknowledgements

I wish to thank the following people most sincerely for contributing to the publication of this book: Mr Fraser Munro of Kennoway Assembly, Fife, for editing the manuscript and making valuable suggestions for its improvement; Dr Donald Cameron for writing the Foreword; my wife, Ruth, for encouraging me to continue writing for the edification of the Lord's people; Mr Graham Stanley of Harehills Assembly, Leeds, for proofreading the text thoroughly prior to its printing; and the staff at John Ritchie Ltd for their work of composition and printing. Without their help, the book would not have been as valuable and accurate as it now is. To God be the glory for His enabling grace to all who have become involved in its production!

Leeds, February, 2018

Contents

Acknowledgements	6
Foreword	9
Select Bibliography	11
General Introduction	13

Joel, the Prophet who Saw the Day of the Lord
Introduction to Joel's Prophecy — 15
Concise Commentary on Joel
Chapter 1 — 25
Chapter 2 — 30
Chapter 3 — 36

Amos, the Prophet who Preached Practical Righteousness
Introduction to Amos' Prophecy — 42
Concise Commentary on Amos
Chapter 1 — 51
Chapter 2 — 60
Chapter 3 — 65
Chapter 4 — 69
Chapter 5 — 73
Chapter 6 — 81
Chapter 7 — 86
Chapter 8 — 93
Chapter 9 — 96

Obadiah, the Prophet who Condemned Edom's Pride and Anti-Semitism
    Introduction to Obadiah's Prophecy   106
Concise Commentary on Obadiah
    Chapter 1   113

Jonah, the Most Successful, yet Most Disobedient, Prophet
    Introduction to the Book of Jonah   124
Concise Commentary on the Book of Jonah
    Chapter 1   134
    Chapter 2   141
    Chapter 3   145
    Chapter 4   149

Micah, the Prophet who Predicted Christ's Birth and Israel's Final Salvation
    Introduction to Micah's Prophecy   156
Concise Commentary on Micah
    Chapter 1   168
    Chapter 2   173
    Chapter 3   177
    Chapter 4   182
    Chapter 5   187
    Chapter 6   192
    Chapter 7   197

Conclusion   204

Foreword

Having made extensive use of Malcolm Davis's concise commentaries, I count it a privilege to be asked to write this Foreword.

Malcolm has the gift of being scholarly without being highbrow or heavyweight. He has already written commentaries on Minor Prophets Hosea and Zechariah; this is his first volume covering five of the remaining ten. This book should be appreciated equally by preacher, teacher, student, eschatologist or simply for personal devotion.

The book is addressed primarily to believers, and as such it is both refreshing and challenging. Indeed, reading through the printer's proofs, I found myself being challenged, as time and again I was reminded that the spiritual problems of God's people with which the Minor Prophets dealt were fundamentally the same as we face in today's increasingly decadent and rebellious society. I quote: "exposing our true spiritual condition before our Lord, and showing us the way to live a more consistent Christian life." This book is Christocentric and well-balanced.

Because each Minor Prophet has his own particular background, style and purpose, Malcolm has not tried to achieve a totally uniform layout. Within their writings we are told a great deal about some of these twelve authors and practically nothing about others. However he reminds us that it is the Holy Spirit who chose what should be included and what excluded, so he does not display the frustration of which some commentators are guilty, by complaining when answers are not immediately forthcoming.

He makes it clear what can be confirmed as factual, giving the appropriate authority, such as quotations by other prophets, historical books or New Testament writers, and what is merely reasonable to assume.

Many of the commentaries in my possession plunge straight into the opening chapter of the book under review. The result is that one can find a mixture of history, authorship identity and the actual message. Malcolm avoids this potential confusion by giving for each book a lengthy Introduction, with carefully labelled sections, before going through the book chapter by chapter. As a Semitic languages expert, he, as a Gentile commentator, has interesting information to give regarding each prophet's style. Within his concise chapter-by-chapter commentaries labelling is precise. One immediately knows which section, verse or group of verses is being expounded.

Although the twelve Minor Prophets are noted for their "foretelling" as well as "forthtelling", the predictive prophecy of each has a different balance of what is short- or medium term prophecy, what is First Coming, and what is Second Coming and Millennial. Not all Minor Prophets deal with all of these.

I look forward to the second volume, covering Nahum to Malachi, less of course Zechariah. Malcolm and I share the conviction that our Saviour's return FOR us cannot be far away. This would be a profitable book for anyone 'left behind' to discover and treasure.

Donald CB Cameron,
Selkirkshire,
March 2018

Select Bibliography

In writing this commentary I have found the following books especially helpful:

Baxter, J. Sidlow. *Explore the Book, 6 vols. in 1.* Grand Rapids, Michigan: Zondervan, 1966.

The Bible Knowledge Commentary: Old Testament. Editors: John F. Walvoord and Roy B. Zuck. Victor Books, 1985.

Cameron, Donald C. B. *The Minor Prophets and the End Times.* Kilmarnock: John Ritchie Ltd, 2010.

Feinberg, Charles Lee. *The Minor Prophets.* Chicago: Moody Press, 1976.

Jensen, Irving L. *Jensen's Survey of the Old Testament.* Chicago: Moody Press, 1978.

The King James Study Bible, King James Version. Nashville, Tennessee: Thomas Nelson, 1988.

MacArthur, John. *The MacArthur Bible Commentary.* Nashville, Tennessee: Thomas Nelson, 2005.

Riddle, John. *Hosea, Joel, Amos, Obadiah.* Kilmarnock: John Ritchie Ltd, 2017.

Tatford, Fredk A. *Minor Prophets, in 4 vols.* Kilmarnock: John Ritchie Ltd, 2014-15. Republished.

Unger, Merrill F. *Unger's Commentary on the Old Testament.* Chattanooga, Tennessee: AMG Publishers, 2002.

What the Bible Teaches, Daniel-Micah. (Ritchie Old Testament Commentaries) Kilmarnock: John Ritchie Ltd, 2011.

General Introduction

This two-volume work aims to cover all the Minor Prophetical books of the Old Testament which have not been included in my other publications on the prophetical books of Scripture as a whole. Both Hosea and Zechariah have been the subject of previously published separate books, entitled *'Israel's Brokenhearted Prophet'* (2017) and *'When the LORD Remembers His Own'* (2014); that is the reason why they are omitted from the present books. Haggai and Malachi will be included in the second volume, despite the fact that they were included in my overview entitled *'Coming Back from Exile'*, issued by Precious Seed Publications in 2015, but I will comment on them in greater detail than I did in the former book.

The present books follow the same policy as is followed in my other commentaries, namely, to explain the meaning of these interesting, but sometimes difficult, small prophecies as concisely as possible and in everyday English. Their anticipated readership is the average Christian who probably has very limited time for study, apart from the Scriptures themselves, because their lives are so busy. Valued feedback from readers of my other books suggests that they are meeting a real need amongst the people of God for intelligible, although not simplistic, explanations of the more obscure parts of the Bible. Practical application is purposely included throughout the commentaries, because prophecy was always intended to correct our moral and spiritual lives when we have begun to depart from the ways of God, and then to assure us of present and future blessing when we have repented and returned to Him. As in my other books, these two volumes are written from the conservative, pre-millennial, pre-tribulational, and dispensational standpoint, since I believe that this alone adequately explains every part of the Bible as a whole.

The prophetical books of Scripture are said by the apostle Peter in his second letter chapter one to be like a light that shines in a dark place, and certainly our contemporary world has become a very dark place both morally and spiritually, just as ancient Israel's world had become apostate and wilfully blind to the light of the LORD's revelation to them. These ancient short prophecies stand like a lighthouse on a rock to warn unwary sailors of hidden reefs in a wild sea, and to point the way to safety in the nearby harbour. The cover designs on these two volumes are intended to illustrate these twin truths very vividly. May the searchlight of these often neglected Minor Prophets illuminate our hearts today, as they did those of the LORD's ancient people Israel over two thousand years ago, exposing our true spiritual condition before our Lord, and showing us the way to live a more consistent Christian life. Above all, may they point us always to Christ as the answer to all our spiritual ills, and to His future Millennial Kingdom as the sphere in which He will one day be acknowledged as this troubled world's KING OF KINGS AND LORD OF LORDS! The faithful remnant of Israel were then waiting for Christ to come the first time in humility to die for their sins on the cross, before He would take up His glorious kingdom and reign without a rival. Christians today are waiting for His imminent coming to the air to rapture us all up to heaven before He begins to open the seals of His judgement on a wicked world in the Tribulation. If the latter time is not far ahead, as many true believers think, how much nearer must be His coming for His blood-bought Church! We unite our hearts with that of the apostle John, who prayed at the end of his writings, 'Even so, come, Lord Jesus', Revelation 22. 20! Maranatha!

Joel, the Prophet who Saw the Day of the LORD

Introduction to Joel's Prophecy

Its Canonical Setting

In the Hebrew book of the twelve Minor Prophets, which were always grouped together and in the same order as is found in our English Bibles, Joel is placed second, after Hosea and before Amos. The overall order of the Minor Prophets is certainly broadly chronological, but probably not exactly so. However, this position of Joel within the so-called 'Twelve' does suggest that it was one of the earliest of the Minor Prophets to be written, and not one of the later ones. More than this we cannot dogmatically prove.

Its Historical Background

The only past event described in the prophecy is a devastating locust plague in the land of Judah, according to chapter 1. Yet this is not related to any king's reign, nor to any other known historical event recorded in the Old Testament. In the first verse of the book, we are left guessing when 'Joel, the son of Pethuel' lived. Evidently, God the Holy Spirit who inspired Joel to write did not intend us to know the precise details of the prophecy's origin and background; His message to His people then and to us today is more important to consider.

Certain features of the book may suggest the possible time when Joel wrote it, although we cannot be at all sure about this. In fact, various dates and periods of Judah's history have been suggested for its composition, ranging from the early pre-exilic period, the ninth century BC, through the later pre-exilic period, right down to the post-exilic period, after the sixth century BC.

We cannot therefore be dogmatic about our own suggestions, but should concentrate on understanding the main message of the book.

However, some Bible scholars note the complete absence from the book of any reference to the later great powers in the Middle East, namely, Assyria and Babylon, and conclude, perhaps rightly, that Joel must have lived before these empires had risen to prominence in the region, namely, in the ninth century BC. Surely, if he had written later than this, he would have mentioned them by name, as they are frequently mentioned in other prophetical books. Consider, too, the remarkable absence from the book of any reference to, or condemnation of, Israel's later idolatry, social injustice, or rampant immorality. There is simply, in the first chapter, a reference to drunkenness. Perhaps, therefore, Joel wrote before the later serious sins had become prevalent in the nation. Certainly, Joel exhorts his fellow-citizens to sincerity and earnestness in their worship of the LORD and their seeking of His help. Perhaps, therefore, there were simply signs in the nation of empty formality and hypocrisy in their worship, which later prophets so soundly condemned. Was Judah simply affected by a spirit of materialism and affluence at the time, and needed this wake-up call from the LORD through Joel to arrest their further spiritual decline into disaster?

We cannot be dogmatic about all this, but some reputable commentators do suggest that Joel may have written during the early part of the reign of the young king Joash in the ninth century BC, when Athaliah, the wicked daughter of Ahab, was ruling Judah so wrongly. Now Joash ruled Judah between about 837-800 BC, so that, if this suggestion is right, Joel may have written his prophecy during the early part of his reign, or during the 830s BC, the later ninth century BC. However, we cannot be at all sure about this tentative conclusion. The book's message is more important to understand than its precise provenance.

Its Author

Joel shares his name with fourteen other men in the Old Testament. It means 'The LORD (Jehovah) is God', which is very similar to Elijah's name, which means 'My God is the LORD'. However, whereas Elijah ministered to the northern kingdom of Israel, Joel clearly ministered to the southern kingdom of Judah, since the book refers to Zion, Judah, Jerusalem, and the valley of Jehoshaphat, and not at all to cities or people in the northern kingdom. Joel exhorts the priests to lead the nation in a sincere expression of repentance, which may mean that he was not himself a priest. We do not know which tribe he was born into; the first verse of his book simply says that he was the son of Pethuel, which means 'Enlarged by God'. It is probable that he was a citizen of the southern kingdom, not a native of the northern kingdom, whom the LORD had sent to prophesy in Judah. Not every prophet was called to minister to his own part of the divided kingdom. Amos, for instance, a native of Tekoa in the southern kingdom, was sent to prophesy to the northern kingdom, as we shall see in the next section of this series of studies. There is every indication here that Joel was probably a native of Judah and sent to prophesy to his own people. It is thought by many Bible students that he was one of the earliest of the writing prophets in Israel, probably earlier than either Hosea or Amos, between whose books his short prophecy is sandwiched.

Its Language and Characteristics

The vast majority of Joel's prophecy is written in fine and regular Hebrew poetry, except for the first verse of chapter one and verses 4 to 8 of chapter 3, which are prose. This is how most more recent translations of the book present it, as they do all the other poetical passages in the Old Testament. It has the advantage of enabling the modern reader to appreciate better the highly emotional style of Joel's writing, his rich imagery, and vivid descriptions, both of the devastating locust plagues with which the LORD chastised His erring people, and of the prediction of His gracious restoration of their sad condition under discipline after their true repentance. Frequently Joel employs repetition of key words to emphasise his message, and there are many examples of synonyms used to good effect. Several imperative commands add a sense of urgency to arrest the attention of his readers, and the book shows careful design and balance in the presentation of its message. As the outline followed below will demonstrate, the prophecy is divided into two equal halves, each of which contains exactly thirty-six verses. From a literary point of view, the book is a gem.

Its Quotations in Scripture

There are a few verses in Joel's prophecy which are either directly quoted, or at least alluded to, in some of the later Old Testament prophets, and it is likely that the quotation is that way round, not the reverse. For instance, Amos appears in his first chapter verse 2 to quote from Joel chapter 3 verse 16, when he says that 'the LORD will roar from Zion, and utter His voice from Jerusalem'. Furthermore, both Isaiah and Micah appear to be alluding to the book of Joel, when they predict that in Christ's Millennial Kingdom the nations 'shall beat their swords into plowshares, and their spears into pruninghooks' (Isaiah 2. 4 and Micah 4. 3), since Joel uses the same language, but in reverse, to describe the nations' frenetic preparation to fight against the LORD in his chapter 3 verse 10, thus, 'Beat your plowshares into swords, and your pruninghooks into spears'. The later exilic prophet Ezekiel follows Joel in predicting that a supernatural river will issue from the threshold of the Millennial Temple, and flow eastwards down to refresh the stagnant waters of the Dead Sea (Ezekiel 47 verses 1 and 8), for Joel chapter 3 verse 18 predicts that this river, 'shall come forth of the house of the Lord, and shall water the valley of Shittim', which is the location of the Dead Sea.

Besides these more direct citations of Joel's prophecy, we should note that the record in the first chapter of the complete devastation caused in the land of Judah by the recent locust plague is seen by the prophet to be a direct fulfilment of the LORD's warning in Deuteronomy chapter 28 that disobedience to His law would bring just such a curse upon His people Israel; see verses 38 and 42.

Turning now to quotations of, or allusions to, Joel in the New Testament, it is very instructive to observe how the apostles used parts of this prophecy in their sermons or writings. First, Peter on the day of Pentecost quoted this prophecy of Joel, saying that the outpouring of the Holy Spirit then was in some

Introduction to Joel's Prophecy

way a fulfilment of Joel chapter 2 verses 28 to 32. Although Peter introduced his sermon by asserting 'this is that', yet it was only a partial fulfilment of this passage, rather than a final and complete fulfilment, as we will explain in the commentary below. Nevertheless, Peter was inspired to recognise that there was a clear correspondence between what Joel predicted and the events at the birth of the New Testament Church. Also, Peter both opened his sermon then by quoting Joel chapter 2 verse 32a, 'Whosoever shall call on the name of the LORD shall be saved' (Acts 2. 21), and concluded his appeal with another reference to it, in the words, 'for the promise is unto you, and to your children, and to all that are afar off, even as many as the Lord our God shall call' (Acts 2. 39).

The apostle Paul also refers to the same grand gospel text quoted above in Romans chapter 10 verse 13 when he is emphasising the universal availability of salvation by faith in Christ, who is here equated with the LORD of the text in Joel, thus proving Christ's Deity.

Finally, the apostle John in the book of Revelation twice alludes to parts of Joel's prophecy. First, in chapter 9, where the description of the demonic locust plague with which the Lord will afflict unbelievers during the first woe of the Trumpet Judgements of the Tribulation, is very similar to Joel's description in his chapter 2 verses 1 to 11 of the locust army which the LORD predicts that He will send against His erring people Judah. Secondly, in Revelation chapter 14 verses 17 to 20, John's description of the Lord putting His sickle of judgement into the winepress of the wrath of God is drawn clearly from the wording of Joel chapter 3 verse 13, 'Put ye in the sickle, for the harvest is ripe: come, get you down; for the press is full, the fats (that is, the vats) overflow; for their wickedness is great'.

Its Outline

Here we draw on two somewhat different outlines by contemporary Bible teachers which both emphasise the main message of the prophecy. First, that given in the MacArthur Bible Commentary, p. 985, thus:

i. Day of the Lord Experienced:

Historical (1:1-20)

    A. Source of the Message (1:1)
    B. Command to Contemplate the Devastation (1:2-4)
    C. Completeness of the Devastation (1:5-12)
    D. Call to Repent in Light of the Devastation (1:13-20)

ii. Day of the Lord Illustrated:

Transitional (2:1-17)

    A. Alarm Sounds (2:1)
    B. Army Invades (2:2-11)
    C. Admonition to Repent (2:12-17)

iii. Day of the Lord Described:

Eschatological (2:18-3: 21)

    A. Introduction (2:18-20)
    B. Material Restoration (2:21-27)
    C. Spiritual Restoration (2:28-32)
    D. National Restoration (3:1 -21)

The second outline is taken from David Gilliland's classic commentary on the book in *What the Bible Teaches, Daniel to Micah*, 2011, p. 288:

Title: 1. 1   **The Authority of Joel**

Part I: 1. 2-2. 17   **The Agony of Judah**
(36 verses)   *The Calamity of the initial Invasion – 1. 2-20*
                             The commands to listen – vv. 2-4
                             The calls to lament – vv. 5-14
                             The cry to the Lord – vv. 15-20

                     The Severity of the imminent Invasion – 2. 1-11
                             Its coming – vv. 1-2
                             Its characteristics – vv. 3-10
                             Its commander – v. 11

Introduction to Joel's Prophecy

The Possibility of the immediate Evasion – 2. 12-17
    The conversion – vv. 12-13
    The caution – v. 14
    The convention – vv. 15-17

Part II: 2. 18-3. 21 The Answer of Jehovah
(36 verses)   *The Immediate Answer – ch. 2. 18-27*
    The removal of the foe – vv. 18-20
    The reversal of the famine – vv. 21-24
    The renewal of the future – vv. 25-27

The Ultimate Answer – 2. 28-3. 21
    The revelation by the Spirit – 2. 28-32
    The retribution on the sinners – 3. 1-17
    The restoration of the supplies – 3. 18-21

From these different outlines two facts are immediately clear: first, that the main subject of Joel's prophecy is the Day of the LORD; secondly, that this short book is divided very evenly in the middle between the devastation which such a time of divine intervention causes and the complete restoration of the situation brought about by the LORD in answer to His people's repentance. Thus they lead us on, finally, to consider the main message of the book.

Its Main Searching Message

If, therefore, the main subject of Joel's prophecy is the Day of the LORD, since the phrase is found five times within the book, at chapter 1 verse 15, chapter 2 verses 1, 11, and 31, and at chapter 3 verse 14, we need to understand what the searching message of the book is, both for the LORD's ancient people Judah and Israel, and also for ourselves today. What is 'the Day of the LORD', what relevance had it for ancient Israel, and what possible relevance has it for us today, well over two thousand years later?

In Scripture the thought behind the phrase 'the Day of the LORD' is that God is intervening directly in the affairs of this world to assert His authority, either in blessing or in judgement. This has happened already at certain critical times, both in the history of Israel and of the Gentile nations, but it will also happen fully and finally in the future, when God intervenes first in judgement during the coming Tribulation, then in both judgement and blessing during Christ's glorious second coming to earth to reign for a thousand years over the whole world in righteousness and peace, the so-called Millennial Kingdom. The Day of the LORD is always a time when God puts things right, and the final Day of the LORD, which will last 1007 years, will be the time when God finally puts the whole world right, after mankind have, in their rebellion against Him, almost completely destroyed it during the so-called 'Times of the Gentiles', which are the times in which we live today.

Thus, sometimes in Scripture 'the Day of the LORD' refers to a critical time of God's judgement during Old Testament history, either on His wayward people Israel, or on some of their neighbouring countries. However, other Scriptures can only refer to the coming future climactic 'Day of the LORD', either the Tribulation judgements, or Christ's glorious Millennial Kingdom. In Joel's Prophecy, there are examples of both these senses of the phrase. First, the contemporary devastating locust plague so vividly described in chapter 1 is clearly called a 'Day of the LORD', a contemporary historical judgement on His people Judah's sins. It seems also to foreshadow the greater climactic judgements of the future Day of the LORD in the end times; see chapter 1 verse 15.

This is certainly true in chapter 2 verses 1 to 11. Here there are divergent views as to whether Joel is simply describing another coming locust invasion, or whether he is predicting a future invasion of Judah by literal armies of the Gentile nations, but under the figure of another locust plague. As we shall see in the following commentary, there is some reason to believe, on the basis of the wording of chapter 2 verse 20, that there is some truth in the latter view, although the earlier description of a locust invasion may also be intended to be understood quite literally as another locust plague. It has been said that coming events do cast their shadows before them, and this is surely true here, whichever future enemy of Israel is being alluded to.

Introduction to Joel's Prophecy

At the end of chapter 2, the reference to the great and terrible day of the LORD can only refer to the climactic judgements at the end of the future Tribulation, while the final reference in chapter 3 verse 14 clearly predicts the decisive final battle of Armageddon. However, the closely associated phrase 'in that day' in chapter 3 verse 18 just as clearly refers to the multiplied blessings which will be bestowed on Israel during the subsequent Millennial Kingdom.

A very prominent theme of Joel's message to his people, therefore, is that they need to repent of their sins in view of the imminence of the Day of the LORD, when they will be judged for them. If they do so, then the LORD will pour out upon them His multiplied blessings, and even restore to them the years that the locust has eaten, by His sovereign overruling power and in a way that we, and they, cannot possibly imagine, see chapter 2 verse 25. The message for us today is similar, and most reassuring. Are we at all conscious of having grown cold in heart towards our Lord, like Judah of old? Although we may not yet have fallen into very grievous sins, as was perhaps true of Judah in Joel's day, still we need to take stock of our spiritual lives, to repent of all known sins, and to 'do the first works', out of 'first love' for Christ, as He expects of us all; see Revelation 2 verses 1 to 7. Otherwise, He will remove our lampstand of effective witness to Him, and we will suffer loss at His judgement seat.

Joel says much about the Holy Spirit and His power and blessing. He predicts a day, the millennial day, when all mankind who survive the Tribulation judgements will be indwelt and empowered by the Holy Spirit. Peter pointed out that the day of Pentecost, the formation of the New Testament Church, anticipated that day, and partially fulfilled the promise in Joel. We believers today are so blessed to be indwelt by the Spirit of God, because He enables us to enjoy fellowship with divine Persons, and to fulfil God's will in a way that not many Old Testament saints were able to do.

If we are correct about the early date of Joel in the ninth century BC, he was probably the earliest prophet to write about the Day of the LORD. In fact, He actually saw it, both in the contemporary history of his people Judah, and in vision concerning the predicted future. Other Old Testament prophets, from Isaiah to Malachi, also predicted this climactic Day of the LORD, when He will ultimately right all wrongs in this world corrupted by man's sin. It was their watchword as they fulfilled their task as Israel's watchmen.

We Christians today can see the way in which the world is going, towards a crisis that will, without the Lord's intervention, end in complete disaster. We need to wake up to our responsibilities as the Lord's watchmen, and to urge our fellow-travellers to eternity to repent of their sins, as we did of ours at our conversions, and to believe the gospel of the grace of God in Christ, since that is our only hope of salvation and eternal life. Perhaps we ourselves need to repent of our sins as believers, even if only of our slothfulness and apathy concerning the work of the Lord in our world, and to live constantly in the light of our day of review, the judgement seat of Christ. Then we can be assured of a full blessing and reward for our lives of service here, and anticipate our Saviour's commendation, 'Well done, thou good and faithful servant: thou hast been faithful over a few things, I will make thee ruler over many things: enter thou into the joy of thy lord!', Matthew 25. 21 and 23. Are we today really ready to take up our responsibilities in Christ's coming kingdom, and to enjoy His blessing for eternity, after a life here of faithful, if perhaps difficult, service for Him now? This is the searching message from Joel's prophecy for all true Christians today!

Concise Commentary on Joel

Joel Chapter 1

1. *Introduction to the LORD's message through Joel, verses 1-3.*

The introduction to the LORD's arresting message given to Joel is as brief as it is important. Only his father's name is mentioned, which serves to distinguish him from all the other Joels in the Old Testament. However, the LORD evidently knew 'Joel the son of Pethuel' to be a faithful man of God, who was spiritually and morally qualified to communicate His inspired and searching message to His wayward people Judah. Judah needed a wake-up call, before they slid further away from their loving covenant Lord GOD, and the LORD had prepared this humble servant Joel as His watchman to encourage their repentance and restoration. The question surely comes to us today in the early twenty-first century AD: 'Are we ready and willing to be our Lord's faithful servants to bring His message to our own contemporaries who are living far away from their Creator God, careless of His claims upon them by creation and redemption?' Has a clear 'word of the LORD' ever come to us to communicate to others around us, and how have we so far responded to His voice to us?

Joel summoned all his fellow-citizens in his part of the Divided Kingdom, but especially the old men, or perhaps the responsible 'elders' in Israel, to listen attentively to the urgent message that the LORD had given to him to pass on to them. In fact, he said that the message was a divine explanation of a unique and devastating event that had evidently recently taken place in Judah. Nothing quite like it had ever happened before in the history of his nation to that day. Why had Judah been allowed by their God to suffer such a devastating and humiliating event as this enormous, and perhaps repeated, plague of locusts? Locust plagues were quite common in the whole Middle East region, and they always caused great harm to the crops and vegetation where they attacked, but this one, or perhaps this series of plagues, was much worse than usual, and the LORD's own people had suffered directly as a result of it. What was the reason for it? His people must listen to the LORD explaining this through His servant Joel, who was His messenger to them.

His message was to be communicated not only to his contemporaries, but also to all the coming generations of their children, so that the whole people might learn the lessons which their covenant LORD was teaching them through it, respond to them, and avoid their ancestors' mistakes and sins. There is a right and godly tradition of doctrine and practice to pass on to faithful men who will teach others also, as the aged Apostle Paul exhorted Timothy, his son in the faith, just prior to his own martyrdom for his faith, 2 Timothy 2. 2. Thankfully, this golden chain of divine testimony has now reached us today in what are probably the closing decades of the Age of Grace, and we are responsible in our turn to transmit it faithfully to our younger saints. What a privilege is ours, like Joel's and the twelve apostles', for these are the true oracles of God! Who is sufficient for these things? Our sufficiency is of God alone.

2. Account of the devastation left in the land after a severe plague of locusts had invaded Judah, verses 4-12.

Now follows a sad account of the complete devastation that these locust invasions had left behind them. However we understand the various names given to locusts in verse 4, we can say of the verse, 'locusts, locusts everywhere, but not a bite to eat!' Some scholars think that Joel is describing successive stages in the development of the locust, whereas others think that he is describing them from different standpoints, with no reference to the stages of their growth. However, all this probably misses the point of verse 4, for Joel is surely using four different nouns to describe the locusts in order to emphasise the totality of the destruction which they had caused, four in Scripture often being used to signify completeness and universality. Joel often uses repetition and groups of synonyms to hammer home his message, which was that these locust invasions were a judgement sent by the LORD against His erring people, in accordance with the covenant curses for disobedience predicted through Moses in Deuteronomy chapter 28.

In verses 5-12, Joel calls on certain members of his nation to wake up to their sad situation and mourn for it, with a view to realising the reason why it had happened. In verses 5 to 7, he first addresses the drunkards among his people, those who had indulged their love of new wine to excess, because the locusts had cut off their source of pleasure completely by eating all the vines. We should notice that the LORD actually calls the land of Israel 'My land', the vines 'My vine', and the fig tree 'My fig tree'. Israel always needed to remember that their Promised Land belonged, first and foremost, to the LORD who had redeemed them to possess it, and they were simply His tenants in it, holding and using it for Him. Evidently, some of the nation had abused their trust, and had overindulged themselves in the produce of the land. The LORD's reply to their sin had been to send a veritable nation of locusts against them like strong lions with sharp teeth to chastise them.

Christians today are likewise bought with a price, the precious shed blood of our redeeming Lord and Saviour, Jesus Christ; see 1 Corinthians 6.19-20. We are not our own, we owe God everything we possess from His gracious hand, and should use it for Him as His faithful stewards. Have we also ever betrayed our trust, and misused our Lord's possessions for our own selfish ends? May we repent of such a serious sin!

In verses 8-10, others in Judah were exhorted to lament like a betrothed virgin who had just been bereaved prematurely of her prospective husband in the prime of his youth. Perhaps the most serious effect of the locust invasion had been that it had deprived the LORD Himself of His due meal and drink offerings in the regular temple worship. The priests could not serve Him as they ought to, for the fields of corn, vines, and olives were completely ruined. When things go wrong in our lives, our ability and even desire to give the Lord His due worship and portion inevitably suffers. Be warned, fellow-Christians!

Finally, in verses 11-12, the LORD through Joel addresses the farmers and vine-dressers, who had all lost their entire crops as a result of the locust plague, and even the various fruit trees which would have borne them. In His disciplinary dealings with His people, the LORD had removed from them all their sources of natural joy and gladness. Our God is not 'a hard man', as the unfaithful servant of Matthew chapter 25 verse 24 so wrongly imagined, but a very bountiful and generous God who will not needlessly cause His creatures such suffering and misery. There must always be a valid reason why He withholds His blessings from us. Usually, the reason is our persistent sins against Him and His laws. Today, people in the formerly more privileged Western nations, who have had the light of the Gospel of the Grace of God for many centuries now, should seriously consider why God has allowed them to be afflicted more than previously by recurrent natural disasters. Are they His answer to our flagrant sins against Him, which are now enshrined in wicked laws legislated by our most conservative governments, and encouraged and flaunted openly by so many among us? Readers, be warned! Your God is speaking to you. Are we willing to listen to His word again, or must complete disaster overtake us before we do so?

3. The LORD's call to repentance, because the disaster was really a judgement against His people, a foreshadowing of the future climactic Day of the LORD, verses 13-20.

In this final section of chapter 1, the LORD through Joel once more calls the priests to lead the whole nation in an exercise of sincere repentance, to be expressed in bitter wailing, mourning dress of sackcloth, and preparedness to act positively upon their humble contrition. It was most serious that they could no longer lead the nation in their offerings of worship. The whole population of the LORD's nation should now be involved in crying out to their God in confession of their sins and prayers for restoration of His former blessings. The truth was that this disaster resulting from the repeated locust plagues was an intervention by the LORD in judgement against His wayward people, a historical Old Testament 'Day of the LORD', and verse 15 further indicates that it foreshadowed the cataclysmic judgements which will befall the whole world during the future final Day of the LORD, the coming Tribulation. In other words, worse was still to come one day.

Verses 16 to 18 elaborate on the natural disaster which had overtaken Judah, partly repeating the laments of verses 4 to 12. There was famine in the land; the worship of the temple had been interrupted; all farming equipment had been ruined; and the animals on the farms had no pasture.

What, therefore, was the answer to this sad and hopeless situation? Was there any ray of hope for the LORD's people? Joel decided to turn to the LORD in his despair, to cry to Him in earnest prayer, presenting Him with the desperate problem which faced Judah. Apparently, a further problem had presented itself concerning the LORD's land, drought and resultant fires, which had destroyed the wilderness pasture lands for the animals which relied on them, and had left them without their normal supply of water from the wilderness brooks. Surely, things could hardly become worse than this! Or could they?

Thus chapter 1 both introduces us to the extent of the problems which faced Judah at that time in their history, explains that they were really an act of discipline against their persistent sins, anticipating the future ultimate Day of the LORD, when God will intervene in decisive judgement against all His rebellious creatures, and encourages His people to express humble and sincere repentance of their disobedience to His laws. Today, we need to give heed to the voice of our God in the various disasters which repeatedly beset us now in various parts of the world, and, likewise, to repent of our sins which so offend His holiness. Beyond this, the first chapter does not go. We, therefore, turn to consider chapter 2 to see what further messages the LORD gave His servant Joel to preach to His beloved people Judah, and, through him, to us today.

Joel chapter 2

1. A very graphic description of a further imminent locust plague, which probably foreshadows an invasion by a future northern Gentile army in the ultimate Day of the LORD, vv. 1-11.

Unfortunately, worse was, and is still, to come for the LORD's wayward people. An even more serious disaster was imminent, such that Joel described it as 'the Day of the LORD', probably a foreshadowing of the ultimate future climactic time of divine judgement. That it was another literal locust plague is surely indicated by verse 25 of this chapter, where the LORD's 'great army' is described as 'the locust', 'cankerworm', 'the caterpillar', and 'the palmerworm', as in chapter 1 verse 4. The further disaster was to be of the same kind as that of chapter 1, but even worse than that had been. However, Joel's language in this section is apocalyptic, as is his reference to 'the northern army', or 'the northerner' in verse 20. Therefore, many commentators hold the view that Joel is predicting an invasion by a northern Gentile army in the end times under the figure of another locust plague. Probably, the truth is the other way round: Joel is predicting another imminent locust invasion which is intended to foreshadow a northern enemy of Israel in the end times. Certainly, there are two distinct levels of interpretation here, a nearer one and a farther one, as often occurs in the writings of the prophets. Both aspects of the chapter need to be understood to gain the full truth.

In verses 1-2, Joel tells the watchmen of Zion to blow the ram's horn trumpet in order to raise the alarm in Judah as the coming locust invasion drew near. This day of the LORD, like the ultimate future one, would be a day of trembling, darkness, and clouds. Witnesses of more recent locust invasions confirm that this passage accurately describes the dreadful experience.

The appearance of the locusts resembles little war-horses, which leap over all obstacles and make a great noise as they devour everything in their path. They certainly look like a well-trained army in battle array. They can climb over walls, and enter all the houses in front of them in the city. The earth quakes before them, and they obscure the light of the sun like a dense cloud. It is not surprising, therefore, that some commentators even see here a prediction of the demonic locust-like creatures of the first woe, the fifth Trumpet Judgement, of Revelation chapter 9 verses 1-11. Coming events do cast their shadows before them.

In verse 11, the LORD is spoken about as the commander of His locust army. He is strong, and executes His word, so that none can endure this great and terrible day of the LORD. This coming calamity is His doing, because He is chastising His wayward people Israel.

2. A further call by Joel to the nation to sincerely repent, pleading deliverance on the ground of the LORD's own glory, vv. 12-17.

Nowhere else in Scripture is there a more earnest call by God to heartfelt repentance than He expresses here through His humble servant Joel. He points out that, although the situation is very serious, it is not completely hopeless, provided that the LORD's people sincerely repent of their sins and turn to Him, acknowledging His merciful and gracious character, and praying that He may repent of His threatened judgement, and instead bless them again. God's repentance is always related to our repentance of our sins against Him. If the LORD did remove the threat of judgement, then there could be a resumption of the temple worship which had had to cease. So Joel again called on the priests to blow the ram's horn trumpet, this time in order to call a fast at a sacred assembly. Everyone was to be involved, from the oldest to the youngest, curtailing all joyful activities. Joel exhorted the priests to lead this expression of repentance by pleading that the LORD would spare His people from reproach, lest the surrounding Gentile nations should gain control over them, and lest they should ask, 'Where is Israel's God?' who once redeemed them. Joel realised that the LORD's own glory was at stake in Israel's fate.

3. *At the watershed of the prophecy, the LORD responds to His people's cry of repentance by promising them complete restoration of their prosperity and deliverance from their northern foe, vv. 18-27.*

When Israel points out that the LORD's own glory is at stake in their sad condition, and also gives clear evidence of repentance from their sins, then the LORD immediately responds to them with many gracious promises of restoration. He declares His holy jealousy for His Promised Land, which had been so terribly devastated by the locusts, and His pity for His own chosen earthly people Israel, who had been so badly affected by the disaster. Jealousy in God is always a good characteristic, since He owns and has absolute rights over His whole creation and over His redeemed people, quite unlike ourselves, who are usually jealous in a very bad sense. Now the LORD affirms that He will answer Israel's prayer of repentance and petition by completely restoring to them the corn and the new wine which they had lost in the disaster, so that they will be completely satisfied with His provision for their needs. Further, He will see to it that they are no longer a reproach among the surrounding heathen Gentile nations.

Then in verse 20, the LORD promises to remove the invading army of locusts and drive them into the barren land by the eastern sea, that is, the Dead Sea, and their rearguard into the western sea, that is, the Mediterranean, so that they drown there, and cause a foul smell to arise from their dead bodies. This will be because they have done great, or monstrous, things to the LORD's land and people. Now while all this accurately describes what does often happen to a literal locust plague when it falls into water, the account of their destruction also probably foreshadows the future destruction of the prominent northern invader of Israel in the end times. We know from both Ezekiel chapters 38-39 and from Daniel chapter 11 verses 40 to 45 that the latter-day Assyrian and the armies of Gog and Magog will be destroyed in this way and in these regions. The expression 'the northerner' (literally) is very significant in this context, since usually locust plagues came from the south or east, rather than the north, while foreign invaders of Israel usually came from the north. This strengthens the case for seeing here not only another locust invasion, but also a foreshadowing of an invading Gentile army in the end times.

In the following verses, the LORD tells His chosen land not to fear, but to rejoice, because just as the invader had done great things to them, now the Lord would do compensating great things for them. The domestic animals would no longer suffer, as He would restore to them their natural pastures and sources of water, while the trees would all be restored also. Let the children of Zion rejoice in the LORD their God, because He promised to give them both the normal seasons of rainfall. The threshing-floors would be full of wheat, and the vats full of wine and oil.

In verse 25, the LORD promises that He would restore to them all the years that the locust plagues had destroyed. They had been His great army to chastise them for their sins, but now they would eat in plenty and be satisfied. They would praise the LORD their God for dealing with them so wonderfully, and would not be disappointed in Him, nor be put to shame before their enemies. In His sovereignty the LORD can do this better than we could ever ask or even think possible. His restoring grace is as complete as it is undeserved. Praise His Name!

4. The LORD through Joel predicts the universal outpouring of the Holy Spirit in the end time at the beginning of the Millennial Kingdom, which will be preceded by the deliverance of the faithful remnant from all their enemies, vv. 28-32.

In the Hebrew Bible this whole section forms a separate short chapter on its own, numbered chapter 3, so that chapter 3 in our English Bibles is numbered chapter 4 in the Hebrew. English readers should be aware that the Hebrew Bible is somewhat differently divided into chapters and verses from the divisions followed in our English Bibles. Here the chapter division in the Hebrew Bible is quite appropriate, since Joel is introducing a new subject, although the general subject of Israel's restoration is being continued from chapter 2 verse 18. Now Joel under the inspiration of the Holy Spirit is projected forwards to the beginning of the Millennial Kingdom of Christ, the ultimate future Day of the LORD, the language becomes apocalyptic, and the following chapter continues to predict events in the end times and the Millennium. The future reference of these verses is indicated by the opening phrase, 'and it shall come to pass afterward'. It is the climax of the prophecy that Joel saw. God's 'afterwards', that is, His dealings with us after a time of trial or chastisement for our sins, are always worth experiencing, as they are times of rich blessing.

In this section, Joel, first in verses 28-29, predicts the ultimate regeneration of all believers on earth at the end of the Tribulation by the outpouring of the Holy Spirit upon them, so that they will be all indwelt by Him in the same way as New Testament Christian believers have been today since the Church was formed into the one body of Christ at Pentecost. This will be one of the major blessings of God's New Covenant with redeemed Israel. Christians today have already received these spiritual blessings many years before Israel will do so in the end times. Peter on the Day of Pentecost was inspired to point out to the astonished crowds attending the feast that the events then corresponded in a very significant way with what will happen finally at the beginning of the Millennium. He said, 'This is that which was spoken by the prophet Joel,' Acts 2. 16. However, it is clear that Pentecost was not a complete and final fulfilment of Joel's prophecy, because on the Day of Pentecost certain features and events mentioned in the verses which follow this prediction in Joel were noticeably absent. Although there was a remarkable outpouring of the Holy Spirit upon all believers, there were no disturbances in the heavenly bodies, as are predicted in Joel chapter 2 verses 30-31. Nor was there any remarkable deliverance of a remnant in Zion and Jerusalem from all their enemies, as there will be in the end times at the campaign of Armageddon, as Joel goes on to explain in verse 32 and in chapter 3. No, Pentecost was a partial fulfilment of Joel's prophecy here, but not the final one.

Verses 30-32 chronologically will precede, not follow, the events of verses 28-29. Other parallel scriptures confirm this, notably Zechariah chapters 12-14. Why then does Joel reverse the order of events here? Probably, the explanation is that, having described the blessings which will be bestowed on repentant Israel in verses 18-27, which will culminate in their national regeneration, verses 28-29, Joel now describes the sequence of events which will lead to their receiving these ultimate blessings in verses 30-32. They will result from the cosmic disturbances which will occur 'before the great and notable Day of the LORD come' at the very end of the Tribulation. Also, Israel will then be surrounded on all sides by their enemies, who will be seeking to annihilate them once and for all as a nation, but a faithful remnant of believers among them will call on the Name of the LORD, and be miraculously delivered by the returning Christ as His feet touch the Mount of Olives. Verse 32 with its promise of salvation for whoever calls in faith on the Name of the LORD is quoted several times in the New Testament as an assurance that salvation is available for all who sincerely repent and believe the Gospel of God's Grace today, or in any age.

Joel chapter 3

1. The LORD's retribution upon all Israel's enemies in the end times at the campaign of Armageddon during the Tribulation, vv. 1-17.

In Joel chapter 3, the LORD continues His predictions concerning the ultimate Day of the LORD, and in particular, in verse 1, promises that He will restore the fortunes of His chosen people Judah and Jerusalem. Then in verses 2-8, the LORD predicts the means by which He will bring this about, namely, by judging all the nations who have oppressed Israel for their sins against them. He will do this during the last part of the future Great Tribulation, as Revelation chapter 16 verses 12 to 16 explain under the sixth Bowl (AV 'Vial') Judgement. This is when He allows all the armies of the nations of the world to be gathered together to the campaign of Armageddon by unclean demonic spirits working deceptive miracles, in order to fight against the LORD and His people Israel. They will intend to annihilate the LORD's earthly people, but really it will be the LORD who will be gathering them all there to judge them for their sins. Although we do not know exactly where the valley of Jehoshaphat is in relation to Jerusalem, its significance lies in the meaning of Jehoshaphat's name, namely, 'the LORD judges'. In verse 14, which refers to the same event, this valley is called 'the valley of decision', that is, the LORD's decision to judge all the gathered nations at the campaign of Armageddon. Zechariah chapter 14 verses 1 to 5 refer to the same event also, and predict the opening up of 'a very great valley', through which the surviving remnant of Israel will flee to safety as the LORD returns to the Mount of Olives, and then judges His enemies.

Verses 2b to 8 then give examples of atrocities which the nations of the world have committed over the centuries against

Concise Commentary on Joel chapter 3

the LORD's people Israel, for which He will judge them at Christ's glorious appearing to reign. They have scattered Israel among all the Gentile nations and divided up their Promised Land, which the LORD again points out is primarily 'My land', His land. They have sold Israelite boys and girls into slavery, and used the proceeds to fulfil their own unclean desires. In verses 4 to 6, the LORD condemns Tyre, Sidon, and Philistia for retaliating against His dealings with them, because they had stolen His silver, gold, and precious things and carried them into their own idolatrous temples to use them in the worship of their false gods. They had also sold the people of Judah and Jerusalem into slavery to the Greeks, far from their native land. For these atrocities the LORD threatened that He would retaliate against them, deliver His captive people from the lands of their captivity, and then see that their own sons and daughters would be sold to His people Judah in reprisal, who would then in their turn sell them into slavery to the Sabeans of south Arabia, far from their native lands. What poetic justice this would be! The LORD assured Israel's enemies that He would keep His word concerning this judgement.

Then, in verses 9-17, the LORD taunts His enemies, and urges them to prepare for war, to come and fight against Him, although it is clearly a hopeless cause. As He says in Psalm 2, the LORD who sits in the heavens will laugh at their defiance and hold them in derision, when they think of attempting to fight against Him. How puny their efforts will be, and so easily defeated by the very breath of the returning Christ's mouth! Although they beat their ploughshares into swords, and their pruning-hooks into spears, the exact opposite of what will happen during Christ's Millennial Reign (see Isaiah 2. 4 and Micah 4. 3), it will all be to no avail. In verse 11, the LORD's 'mighty ones', who are summoned to come down, are the angels whom He is sending to execute judgement on the gathered armies, as the LORD judges them all in the valley of Jehoshaphat.

Revelation chapter 14 verses 15 to 19 allude to several parts of verse 13 here, as John sees two visions of the coming judgements during the Tribulation under the twin figures of the wheat harvest and the grape harvest. Mankind will then be fully ripe for final judgement, and the vats of the LORD's righteous wrath will be full, because man's wickedness will be great. The judgement of the grape harvest symbolises the campaign of Armageddon, as Revelation chapter 14 verse 20 makes clear, without actually naming Armageddon there. That verse simply indicates that the war will extend to the whole length of the Promised Land, and the blood which will be shed then will be like the overflowing grape juice of the winepress. There will be millions of soldiers gathered in the so-called 'valley of decision', or the LORD's judgement, for that will be the first part of the ultimate Day of the LORD; the time of climactic judgement upon rebellious mankind.

Verse 15 again predicts disturbances in the heavenly bodies, which chapter 2 verse 31 had previously prophesied in connection with the great and terrible Day of the LORD. Here the LORD says that the usual light derived from the sun and the moon will grow dark, and the brightness of the light from the stars will be diminished. Then verse 16 says that the LORD will roar, like an angry lion, from Zion, and utter His voice from Jerusalem in judgement, so that the heavens and earth will shake, probably referring to the earthquakes which will occur during the Tribulation, in addition to the disturbances in the planets. This part of the verse is probably quoted by the slightly later prophet Amos in chapter 1 verse 2 of his prophecy.

However, the second half of verse 16 commences the other side of the picture which will emerge from the climax of the Tribulation period, namely, Israel's protection, deliverance, and blessings during Christ's Millennial Kingdom. At that time, the LORD will be the hope and shelter of His chosen earthly people Israel, and their strength, or stronghold. Then verse 17, a transitional verse between the verses of judgement and those which promise future blessing, affirms that Israel will know certainly that the LORD their God is dwelling in Zion, always ready to protect and bless His people from His holy mountain. Jerusalem will be holy, separated from all other places and consecrated to the worship and service of the LORD alone. No strangers, or aliens, will ever again pass through His chosen city to molest it. The end of the Tribulation will see the end of Israel's suffering, both from the LORD's chastening hand and from the hands of the surrounding Gentile nations.

2. Finally, the LORD promises to completely restore the prosperity of Israel during the Millennial Kingdom, to judge their enemies, and to cleanse Israel from their sins, vv. 18-21.

Joel now looks on to Israel's final restoration during Christ's future kingdom, when the LORD will dwell in the new Millennial Temple in Jerusalem in the returned Shekinah glory cloud. The Millennial Kingdom will be a time of great blessing, prosperity, and final restoration and cleansing for Israel from all their sins.

In verse 18, the LORD promises that the mountains and hills will become very fertile, and there will be abundant new wine and milk produced from them, the very opposite of what Joel had described in chapters 1 and 2 as a result of the LORD's chastening through the locust plagues. There will no longer be any drought conditions, but the rivers and streams in Judah will flow abundantly with water. The end of this verse predicts the creation of the supernatural river which will flow from the threshold of the new Millennial Temple towards the valley of Shittim, that is, into the Dead Sea, to refresh its waters. Both Ezekiel chapter 47 and Zechariah chapter 14 also refer to this divine river, and Zechariah adds to the description by saying that it will not only flow eastward into the Dead Sea, but also westward into the Mediterranean Sea. Ezekiel states that it will enable fishing to take place in the formerly unproductive waters of the Dead Sea.

By contrast, verse 19 predicts that Israel's and Judah's longstanding enemies, Egypt and Edom, will be a desolate wilderness during the same Millennial Kingdom of Christ, because they had committed violent acts against the children of Judah, shedding much innocent blood in their land over the centuries of their history. However, verse 20 reassures Israel that at that time both Judah and Jerusalem will enjoy complete and permanent security from attack by all their former enemies.

Finally in verse 21, the LORD explains that this will be possible because at that time He 'will cleanse' Israel 'from their blood that I have not cleansed' before then. This has been understood by commentators in several different ways. It could mean, according to F.A. Tatford, that God will 'vindicate His people, who had been massacred by their inveterate foes'. However, more probably, according to John Riddle, it means that they will be cleansed from their guilt so that the LORD may dwell among them, and 'their bloodguilt' may refer to Israel's crowning sin in crucifying Christ, their true Messiah, when He came to them the first time. David Gilliland holds this view. Certainly, Zechariah chapters 12 to 14 more fully predict how the nation will repent upon seeing the same Christ whom they had pierced coming to them to deliver them from all their enemies at the end of the Tribulation. They foretell how Israel will mourn for Him, but be cleansed from their sins by the blood of Christ shed for them on Calvary, and then be completely restored to their LORD God and blessed in the Millennial Kingdom. The LORD through Joel promises this here much more briefly. The evidence that they have been totally cleansed will be the fact that the LORD will be once more dwelling in Zion in their very midst, after centuries of absence and estrangement due their persistent sins. Now, however, the matter will be considered completely and finally settled. Israel will one day be fully restored to their God.

Thus, Joel's prophecy, which began on a very sad, agonised, and low note, ends on a very high, hopeful, and joyful note, as the prophet sees with the eye of faith the ultimate restoration and blessing of his wayward people, Israel and Judah, in the ultimate Day of the LORD, after their long history of failure and divine chastisement. True and thorough repentance was the key to their recovery and blessing. This can be true of us too, especially if we are conscious of having failed our gracious Lord in any particular way, as Israel have done. God is far more ready and willing to restore us and bless us again spiritually than we are to repent, to confess our sins to Him, and to forsake them decisively. This is the searching message that the little prophecy of Joel brings to us today.

AMOS

Amos, the Prophet who Preached Practical Righteousness

Introduction to Amos' Prophecy

Its Canonical Setting
In the traditional order of the Hebrew books of the Twelve Minor Prophets, Amos has always been placed third, after Hosea and Joel, and before Obadiah and Jonah. Hosea was probably a contemporary of Amos, and may have outlived him, while Joel could have lived before them both. We do not now know the reasons for the precise ordering of the Minor Prophets.

Its Historical Background
The Prophecy of Amos can be dated fairly certainly to sometime during the second quarter of the eighth century BC, because Amos states that he prophesied during the reigns of Uzziah, king of Judah (ca. 790-739 BC), and Jeroboam II, king of Israel (ca. 793-753 BC), two years before a memorable earthquake which is also mentioned in Zechariah chapter 14 verse 5. We do not know the exact date of this earthquake, but since Israel was evidently enjoying a period of great prosperity at the time when Amos wrote, it is likely that he wrote in about the middle of the sole reigns of Jeroboam II and Uzziah, who were both able to expand their nations' borders, due to the contemporary weakness of the Assyrian Empire. Thus Amos may have written his book in about 760 BC. This date is suggested in the *New Bible Dictionary*.

Politically, therefore, Amos lived during a time of great affluence and prosperity, especially in the Northern Kingdom under the stable rule of Jeroboam II, who, following the lead of

Introduction to Amos' Prophecy

his father Jehoash (2 Kings 13. 25), restored much of the original territory of Israel, according to a prophetic utterance by Jonah, see 2 Kings 14. 25. This period was also a time of peace with Judah under Uzziah, and their more distant neighbours. Morally and spiritually, however, it was a time of great corruption, moral depravity, and spiritual perversion, against which Amos was inspired to preach fearlessly. The wealth which had come to Israel as a result of Jeroboam's conquests had not been distributed fairly, and the rich had become richer, and had oppressed the poor so that they had become poorer. There was not only social injustice, but also judicial injustice, and the poor had often become slaves of the rich. In his preaching, Amos was led to emphasise practical righteousness, which had sadly been ignored.

Further, the social conditions in the nation had affected their practice of religion, which had been seriously corrupted from the time when Jeroboam I first set up the idolatrous calf-images at Bethel and Dan as substitute centres of worship for the true worship of the LORD at Solomon's Temple in Jerusalem. Although ritual sacrifices were being maintained at these counterfeit centres, they were permeated with ungodliness, idolatry, and moral depravity. The LORD spoke consistently through Amos to announce His imminent judgement for such spiritual perversion. After a period of tragic decline, political instability, and violence, judgement day came for the Northern Kingdom of Israel in 722 BC at the hands of a revitalised and expanding Assyrian Empire.

Its Author

Amos came from the small village of Tekoa, which was about ten miles south of Jerusalem in the wilderness of Judea, where David had once been persecuted by Saul. He is the only prophet to announce his occupation before declaring his divine commission. In chapter 1 verse 1, he states that he was a sheep farmer, while in chapter 7 verse 14, he adds to this, when speaking to Amaziah, the idolatrous priest of Bethel, that he was a gatherer, or tender, of sycamore fruit. The reason why he said this, particularly to the false priest Amaziah, was that he was making it clear that he had no academic training in the schools of the prophets at the time, nor had he ever thought before that the LORD would call him as His prophet. In other words, he was an uneducated layman, a thoroughgoing countryman, whom the LORD had unexpectedly called to prophesy to His people Israel. As a faithful believer, he saw through all the religious hypocrisy of the Northern Kingdom's idolatrous system of worship, and preached boldly and bluntly against it at its very central shrine, 'the king's chapel' at Bethel.

Amos was a contemporary of both Jonah and Isaiah, as well as of Hosea. Although he was born and bred in the Southern Kingdom of Judah, he ministered chiefly to the Northern Kingdom of Israel, which was the first part of the Divided Kingdom to go into exile, and to become absorbed into the empires of their Gentile neighbours, probably because it was the more corrupt and apostate.

Amos' name means 'burden' or 'burden-bearer', and this provides us with a key to the message of his book. The LORD gave Amos a great burden concerning the national sin of His chosen earthly people Israel and its inevitable result in national judgement and exile.

Its Language and Characteristics

Hebrew Bible scholars tell us that, on the whole, the Hebrew text of the prophecy of Amos has been well-preserved, so that there are fewer difficulties of interpretation and translation to overcome in understanding his messages than there are in some other Old Testament prophetical books.

Sidlow Baxter in his introduction to Amos in *Explore the Book* says that the prophet's writing style is 'distinguished by a peculiar forcefulness and rural freshness', with many illustrations from his native country environment, and that 'there is a clearness and regularity, an elegance and colour and freshness about it, which give it a literary charm all its own'. He was very blunt when confronting the sinful people of the Northern Kingdom, whether the rich and influential, or the false idolatrous priesthood and ruling nobles. For example, who else would dare to address the rich upper-class ladies of Samaria as 'cows', see chapter 4 verse 1?!

However, despite his lack of formal education, Amos has

Introduction to Amos' Prophecy

written a very well-ordered book, quite clear to follow, and easy to analyse, as the sample outlines below will demonstrate.

Its Quotations

First of all, Amos appears in his introduction, in chapter 1 verse 2, to be quoting from Joel chapter 3 verse 16, when he says that, 'the LORD will roar from Zion, and utter His voice from Jerusalem', that is, in judgement. It is probable that the quotation is that way round, and not the reverse. If this is so, then Amos must have prophesied after the time of Joel.

Then, there are two quotations of Amos in the Book of Acts. Firstly, Stephen, in his bold defence to the Jewish Sanhedrin, quoted from Amos chapter 5 verses 25 to 27, 'O ye house of Israel, have ye offered to Me slain beasts and sacrifices by the space of forty years in the wilderness? Yea, ye took up the tabernacle of Moloch, and the star of your god Remphan, figures which ye made to worship them: and I will carry you away beyond Babylon', Acts 7. 42-43. Amos was convicting the Jews of idolatry during the wilderness wanderings, and predicting the later exiles for their sins. Amos actually wrote, 'beyond Damascus', not 'beyond Babylon', but Stephen anticipated and included in his thought the later Babylonian exile of Judah as well as the earlier Assyrian exile.

Secondly, in Acts chapter 15 verses 16 to 17, James alludes to Amos chapter 9 verses 11 to 12 in the Greek Septuagint translation when speaking of God's intention to save Gentiles as well as Jews. We shall discuss the precise significance of this allusion in the concise commentary. James here simply refers to this passage as 'the words of the prophets', thus confirming the place of Amos among them.

Its Outline

The outlines of the Book of Amos selected here are taken from three sources:

Firstly, the brief outline by Jack Hay in the relevant volume of *What the Bible Teaches:*

He says, 'An outline of the book gives us five divisions of varying size'.

1. Introduction (1. 1-2)
2. The Transgressions and Punishment of Eight Nations (1. 3-2. 16)
3. The Guilt and Punishment of Israel Specifically (3. 1-6. 14)
4. The Coming Judgment on Israel Predicted and Illustrated (7.1-9. 10), in which 7. 10-17 is a parenthesis, a record of opposition to the prophet's ministry
5. The future Restoration of the Nation (9. 11-15)

Secondly, the somewhat fuller outline in Sidlow Baxter's *Explore the Book*:

The Book of Amos
Judgment for Abused Privilege

1. Eight 'Burdens' (i-ii).
   Damascus (i. 3); Gaza (6); Tyre (9); Edom (11); Ammon (13); Moab (ii. 1); Judah (4); Israel (6). Note: 'For three transgressions and for four'.

2. Three Sermons (iii-vi).
   Judgment Deserved (iii. 1-10); Decreed (iii. 11-15)).
   Judgment Deserved (iv. 1-11); Decreed (iv. 12-13).
   Judgment Deserved (v. 1-15); Decreed (v. 16-vi.).

3. Five 'Visions' (vii-ix.).
   Grasshoppers (vii. 1); Fire (vii. 4); Plumbline (vii. 7); Summer Fruit (viii.); God over the Altar (ix.). Note the final promise to Israel (ix. 11-15).

Thirdly, the fuller outline in John MacArthur's *The MacArthur Bible Commentary*:

Outline of Amos
i. Judgments Against the Nations (1.1-2. 16)
   A. Introduction (1.1-2)

B. Against Israel's Enemies (1.3-2. 3)
   C. Against Judah (2.4-5)
   D. Against Israel (2.6-16)

ii. Condemnations Against Israel (3.1-6. 14)
   A. Sin of Irresponsibility (3.1-15)
   B. Sin of Idolatry (4.1-13)
   C. Sin of Moral/Ethical Decay (5.1-6. 14)

iii. Visions of Judgment and Restoration (7.1-9. 15)
   A. The Lord Will Spare (7.1-6)
      1. Vision of Locusts (7.1-3)
      2. Vision of Fire (7.4-6)
   B. The Lord Will No Longer Spare (7.7-9. 10)
      1. Vision of the plumb line (7.7-9).
      2. Historical interlude (7.10-17)
      3. Vision of the fruit basket (8.1-14).
      4. Vision of the altar (9.1-10)
   C. The Lord Will Restore (9.11-15)

From all these outlines it will be immediately obvious that the Book of Amos is very clearly arranged. Amos may have been an untrained layman, but he obviously had a very orderly mind. The LORD used him in a remarkable way to bring His message to His erring people. Amos was like many other simple, but faithful, believers before and since whom God has been able to use in His purposes of judgement and grace. This fact should be an encouragement to us today.

Its Main Searching Message

In his prophecy Amos, the humble sheep farmer, is unusually stern and severe. Both Hosea and Amos chiefly addressed the Northern Kingdom of Israel, but their approaches were very different from one another. Whereas Hosea presented his people's sins as an outrage of divine love, Amos spoke of them chiefly as an outrage of divine law. His ministry was one of light, while Hosea's was one of love. Whereas Hosea evidently felt for his wayward people with great sympathy and sorrow, Amos had sympathy chiefly for the oppressed poor among his hearers. Otherwise, he was motivated by a sense of divine righteousness, against which his hearers had seriously offended.

Sidlow Baxter points out that the key to understanding Amos' prophecies of judgement is found in chapter 3 verse 2, which says concerning the LORD's chosen people Israel, 'You only have I known of all the families of the earth: therefore I will punish you for all your iniquities'. Judgement is always determined by God according to privilege granted to us by Him. Greater privilege increases responsibility accordingly, and many times in the Old Testament the LORD and His faithful servants point out and enumerate Israel's great privileges and blessings as His chosen earthly nation right from the time that they were formed into a nation in Egypt. Yet they had sinned persistently against His law and had either neglected or perverted His worship. Their just punishment must therefore be correspondingly greater than that of other nations who had not experienced such privileges from God's hand. The imminent punishment to be meted out to the Northern Kingdom of Israel was the Assyrian Exile in 722 BC, from which God's people would not return before the beginning of Christ's Millennial Kingdom.

This divine principle of judgement applies even today as fully as it did in the days of Amos. Christian believers today are far more blessed with spiritual blessings than ever earthly Israel was. Therefore, our responsibility is even greater than Israel's was to be faithful to our gracious Lord and His word. If we are not faithful, we may expect severe consequences, both in our spiritual lives, in our ordinary circumstances in this world, and in eternity. Let us, then, live grateful and obedient lives to His glory.

Throughout his prophecy Amos preaches the importance of practical righteousness in our daily lives, and in our manner of, and motives for, worshipping the LORD. He abominated the wicked practices that so characterised the people of Israel's dealings with one another and ruined the lives of the poor and less privileged among them. The contemporary affluence and luxury of Jeroboam II's kingdom had led to complete corruption in both business and religion. Often today, material prosperity in a nation, such as

Introduction to Amos' Prophecy

ours in the United Kingdom, has heralded a marked moral and spiritual decline that did not characterise former days of difficulty and poverty. It is a sad fact that no-one today advocates a national day of prayer for the deliverance of our nation from invasion, or any similar dangers, such as terrorist attacks. These days of prayer were called several times, and were well-supported, during the darkest days of the Second World War, and received remarkable providential answers in the progress of that war. Like Israel in Old Testament times, we today as nations have largely forgotten God, and are reaping a terrible harvest of trouble and sorrow.

However, like most of the other Minor and Major Prophets of Israel and Judah, Amos does not end his book on a note of defeat, despair, or condemnation. As in other prophecies, the LORD gives him a glorious vision of Israel's future ultimate restoration and triumph in Christ's Millennial Kingdom, the Day of the LORD. The last five verses of chapter 9 are most encouraging and reassuring that all will not finally be lost for the LORD's grand purposes in and through Israel. The Davidic dynasty and kingdom will be restored, and His people Israel will dwell securely in their own Promised Land at last unmolested and divinely blessed.

Also, it should be pointed out that, in several places in his book, Amos implies, or explicitly states, that, in His exercise of judgement, the LORD is longsuffering, often waiting a long time for repentance to be manifested in His own nation's, or other nations', national lives, before He executes His just judgement against them decisively. In chapter 7, the LORD is seen sparing Israel from immediate judgement in answer to the prophet's own plea, which fact demonstrates that Amos was not a really hard man; rather, he was simply being completely faithful to his commission from the LORD to deliver His message to His beloved people. 'In judgement the LORD remembers mercy' (cf. Habakkuk 3.1) is a permanent principle in Scripture, which proves that 'He does not willingly afflict the children of men' (cf. Lamentations 3.33), however much we deserve it, but really desires to bless us, if only our ways conform to the standards of His own holiness.

In conclusion, therefore, we can say that Amos is the Minor

Prophet who preached an intensely practical righteousness rather more than some others, and that we are meant to learn much about our own practical righteousness from his book in many areas of our lives. He stood apart from the corrupt counterfeit religion of the Northern Kingdom, and severely condemned it. We should do the same with corrupt Christendom around us today, and simply follow the word of God in our local assemblies' lives. Unlike Israel, we should not abuse our great spiritual privileges as the Lord's New Testament Church today in the Age of Grace, or we will suffer greatly for doing this. We have, like Israel, a good spiritual heritage from previous generations of true believers, who sacrificed much to gain it, but we could lose all the benefit of it through pride, disobedience, indifference, or slothfulness. So let us not despise simple, forthright preachers who tell us where we have gone wrong; rather, let us respond in repentance to their exhortations, and seek to change our ways before the Lord. They have our highest good at heart, and, if we do respond positively to their teaching or rebukes, they invariably give us good reasons to hope for restoration and renewed blessings in Christ, based on solid promises in Scripture. Rather, let us value humble, honest men like Amos highly as true ambassadors for our soon-coming Lord. We will not regret it, for 'Faithful are the wounds of a friend' (Proverbs 27.6)!

Concise Commentary on Amos

Amos Chapter 1

1.Introduction to the Prophecy, vv. 1-2.

Amos begins his prophecy by saying that the words which he is writing 'he saw', presumably in a vision from the LORD. This confirms to us that his book is inspired by God, and therefore profitable for many different spiritual purposes; see 2 Timothy 3. 16. Earlier in Israel's history, prophets were called seers. John Riddle refers here to Psalm 89 verse 19, which explains this process, 'Then thou spakest in vision'. The very words which Amos wrote were given to him by the LORD in a vision.

Amos further states that he was one of the 'herdmen of Tekoa', where he uses an unusual word for 'herdmen', namely, *noqed*. M.F. Unger says that this 'suggests that the sheep herded by Amos were not the common variety, but a dwarfed variety, prized for its wool'. In chapter 7, Amos gives further information concerning his humble background and unexpected call by the LORD to prophesy to Israel. His primary commission was to the Northern Kingdom of Israel, although he came from the Southern Kingdom of Judah, but some other nations were included among the recipients of his prophetic messages, as we shall see.

Verse 1 includes a reference to the reigning kings of Judah and Israel during the time of his ministry, namely, Uzziah and Jeroboam the son of Joash, that is, Jeroboam II. This was a time of great prosperity and affluence in both parts of the Divided Kingdom. However, Amos adds the significant fact that he prophesied two years before a very severe earthquake that was long remembered. Probably, he saw this catastrophic event as a divine judgement upon the peoples to whom he was sent to prophesy, thus confirming the truth of his stern messages to them from the LORD, for the sad fact was that the citizens of both Israelite kingdoms had taken advantage of their prosperity and material wealth to engage in all kinds of moral and spiritual evils.

In verse 2, Amos probably quotes part of Joel chapter 3 verse 16, when he says that, 'The LORD will roar from Zion, and utter His voice from Jerusalem', in judgement, but he reverses the meaning of Joel's words in so doing. Joel had predicted that the LORD would one day judge all Israel's enemies for oppressing them previously, but Amos predicts that the LORD will soon judge Israel itself for their many sins against Him. Then the second half of the verse predicts the sad effect of His imminent judgement, which this time would take the form of a severe drought, upon even the areas of Israel which normally remained fertile and well-watered, namely the pastures of the shepherds and the top of Mount Carmel, which means 'the garden land' beside the sea. If even beautiful and fruitful Mount Carmel was to be affected, how much worse would other regions be devastated by the coming judgements? John Riddle points out helpfully that the LORD would speak in judgement from His chosen centre of worship, where alone His Glory-cloud still dwelt, namely, Jerusalem, not from the idolatrous religious centres of Bethel or Dan in the Northern Kingdom of Israel.

2. *The LORD announces judgement upon Damascus in Syria, vv. 3-5.*

Now the LORD through Amos announces severe judgements upon eight different nations for their persistent sins. This whole section, which occupies the first two chapters of the book, should be compared with similar prophecies against foreign nations in Isaiah, Jeremiah, and Ezekiel. However, the arrangement of the indictments in Amos differs from that followed in the other prophetical books. The latter place all the indictments of foreign nations after those directed against Israel. Amos reverses this usual order, placing indictments of Syria, Philistia, and Tyre, nations furthest removed from Israel and unrelated to them, first, then related nations, Edom, Ammon, and Moab, next, and only then does he indict Judah, Israel's brother nation, and finally Israel, who are the main focus of his messages. In this Amos shows great tact, since his hearers in Israel would welcome indictments of their enemies, but not so easily accept indictments against themselves or Judah. He therefore puts his own nation last, in order perhaps to soften the blows he is about to give them.

Another noticeable feature of this catalogue of judgements is the introductory formula, repeated in the case of every nation, 'for three transgressions of..., and for four, I will not turn away the punishment thereof'. It indicates an important principle which the LORD has always followed in His judgement of mankind, and individual nations. This is that there is a limit to the extent to which the LORD will exercise longsuffering with our persistent sins and withhold judgement from us. If we go beyond this limit, which He alone can decide, He will execute judgement against us.

For instance, in Genesis chapter 15, the LORD said to Abram that 'the iniquity of the Amorites' was 'not yet full'; therefore He would not yet execute final judgement against them in the form of annihilation by His people. However, when, many years later in Deuteronomy chapter 7, the LORD was giving the young nation of Israel the command to utterly destroy the Amorites and the Canaanites in the Promised Land, He indicated that there was to be no mercy shown towards them; they were now too wicked and dangerous to His people to be allowed to live. His longsuffering had been exhausted.

This applies to God's dealings with nations today, and to His dealings with all of us individually as well. He is waiting for, and wanting, us to repent, but if we fail to do so, and continue committing serious sins against Him and our fellowmen, He will suddenly execute summary judgement against us. This is consistently the case here in Amos chapters 1 to 2. All these nations had so sinned that the LORD's patience with them had become exhausted, so that He must judge them decisively. In each nation's case, He mentions a crowning sin which finally tipped the balance of the LORD's justice against them, usually being a terrible crime against humanity which called for retribution.

Let us, therefore, turn to consider the LORD's indictment through Amos of Damascus, the beautiful capital city of Syria, perhaps the oldest city in the world. The crime of the Syrians was that they had inflicted indescribable cruelties upon the Israelites who lived in the region of Gilead, east of the River Jordan. They had threshed the inhabitants of Gilead with iron threshing implements. Undoubtedly, the victims of this outrage all died a very painful death. These crimes are recorded in 2 Kings. In chapter 8 verses 11-12, Elisha had predicted that Hazael king of Syria would deal very cruelly with the children of Israel. This prediction was fulfilled, first in chapter 10 verses 32-33, which record that, during the very dubious reign of Jehu, the LORD began to cut Israel short at the hand of Hazael, who smote them from Jordan eastward, 'all the land of Gilead' and Bashan, the territory of the Gadites, the Reubenites, and the Manassites. It was fulfilled again during the later reign of Jehoahaz, according to chapter 13 verses 4-7, when the king of Syria oppressed Israel, 'destroyed them, and had made them like the dust by threshing'.

Verse 4, therefore, predicts the punishment which would be meted out to the house, or dynasty, of Hazael. In His holy wrath the LORD would send a fire of judgement upon them, that is, they would be invaded and destroyed. The palaces of their ruling dynasty, the Ben-hadads, who were the descendants of Hazael, would be devoured by this invasion. This dynasty was a constant oppressor of Israel. Now the LORD would see that they received just retribution for their crimes. Verse 5 predicts that the LORD would see that the gate bar of Damascus was broken through by an enemy, so that the city was invaded, its citizens killed in the valley of Aven, or wickedness, and the king killed in 'the house of Eden', or the house of delight. Then the people left living in Syria would be taken into captivity in a place called Kir, which is unidentified, but, according to Amos chapter 9 verse 7, was the place from which the Syrians originated. Poetic justice indeed!

2 Kings chapter 16 records the fulfilment of this prophecy during the reign of Ahaz, the evil king of Judah, about fifty years later than the time when Amos wrote this. Ahaz requested that Tiglath-pileser, king of Assyria, attack both Rezin, king of Syria, and

Pekah son of Remaliah, king of Israel, who had been threatening to invade Judah. This the king of Assyria did on behalf of Ahaz, and chapter 16 verse 9 records how he attacked Damascus, captured it, carried away its population to a place called Kir, and killed Rezin, the Syrian king. The LORD overruled all the wickedness involved in this event and brought His sovereign purposes of judgement to pass on Syria. He is in absolute control of international events like this, although we may not think so. Yes, our God reigns!

3. *The LORD announces judgement on Gaza in Philistia, vv. 6-8.*

The reference to Gaza here includes all the four Philistine cities within their original Pentapolis, as verse 8 makes clear, since it names the other three, namely, Ashdod, Ashkelon, and Ekron. The fifth city, Gath, is omitted, probably because it had already been destroyed by King Uzziah, according to 2 Chronicles chapter 26 verse 6. Gaza may have been selected here as representative of all the remaining Philistine cities because it was the most southerly of them all, and thus the key to Palestine on the south.

The crowning sin of Gaza had been that they had taken captive an entire population and then handed them over to Edom, who were Israel's most bitter enemy, probably for ill-treatment or slavery. Their victims were probably Israelites, since this incident may be referred to in Joel chapter 3 verses 4-6. There Joel says that the Philistines sold some of the Israelite prisoners to the Phoenicians, who in turn sold them to the Greeks. It had been very profitable to engage in this inhuman slave-trading. Amos may have been referring to the invasion of Judah by the Philistines and the Arabians during the reign of Jehoram, which is recorded in 2 Chronicles chapter 21 verse 16. The fact that this verse states that it was the LORD who stirred up the spirits of these foreign nations against Jehoram because of his wickedness, did not excuse their actions. Two evils never make a right in God's eyes.

In verses 7-8, therefore, the LORD announces the Philistines' punishment, which is again described as a fire, a violent end by invasion. The defensive wall of Gaza, and its palaces, would be destroyed, the inhabitants of Ashdod and the ruler of Ashkelon would be killed, and similar judgement would be meted out to

Ekron. The remainder of the Philistines would then perish, so that Philistia would disappear from the map of the region. Several other Old Testament prophecies predict judgement on Philistia in later times, namely, Jeremiah chapter 47, Zephaniah chapter 2 verse 4, and Zechariah chapter 9 verses 5-7. The latter prophecy is thought to have been fulfilled through the conquests of Alexander the Great in the later fourth century BC.

4. *The LORD announces judgement on Tyre in Phoenicia, vv. 9-10.*

Next, the LORD through Amos announces the fate of the maritime capital of Phoenicia, Tyre, for their part in slave-trading with a whole population of Israelites, and handing them over to their worst enemy, Edom, as mentioned in verse 6 and referred to in Joel chapter 3. They were complicit with the Philistines in perpetrating this atrocity. Their crime was made worse by the fact that Israel had for centuries a brotherly covenant with Tyre, ever since the days of their king Hiram. He had always been a lover of David, and assisted him and Solomon in the construction of the temple in Jerusalem, see 1 Kings chapter 5 and the following chapters. God views the breaking of covenants very seriously, and always holds accountable those who commit this sin. No king of Israel or Judah had ever made war on Phoenicia, but the Phoenicians had betrayed Israel's trust in them.

Again, as with Syria and Philistia, the LORD predicted severe punishment by foreign invasion. This happened twice during the history of Tyre: first, when Nebuchadnezzar besieged the city for thirteen years, between 585 and 573 BC, when the mainland site of the city was destroyed. Secondly, when Alexander the Great destroyed the island part of the city after a much shorter siege in 332 BC. 'The mills of God grind slowly, but they grind exceeding small'! All this was the result of unfaithfulness to their covenant promises to Israel. Are we today faithful and true to our word and solemn promises? Do we always love our fellow-brethren as we should?

5. *The LORD announces judgement on Edom, vv. 11-12.*

As with the preceding announcement of judgement on Tyre, here the LORD is condemning Edom for a gross violation of brotherly love, for Edom's ancestor, Esau, was the twin brother of Jacob, the progenitor of the nation of Israel. The LORD does not appear to refer to any one instance of Edom's hatred of Israel, but affirms that this had been a perpetual feature of his relationship with Israel, because He says that 'he did pursue his brother with the sword, and did cast off all pity, and his anger did tear perpetually, and he kept his wrath for ever'; a terrible state of mind, soul, and spirit to foster. Edom had a vendetta against Israel. This came to the fore when the Babylonians destroyed Jerusalem in 586 BC. They encouraged the invaders in their dreadful task, and rejoiced over Israel's fall and exile. They were also involved in the same instance of slave-trading with Israelite prisoners as is probably referred to in the condemnations of Gaza and Tyre.

By way of contrast, the Israelites, when travelling through the wilderness on their way to their Promised Land, were strictly forbidden to attack, or meddle with, any of the Edomites, precisely because the LORD regarded Edom as the brother of Israel, and therefore to be treated with respect, brotherly love, and forbearance. This charitable attitude, commanded by the LORD Himself, was not reciprocated by the Edomites.

We today need to ask ourselves whether there is anyone, fellow-believer, or non-Christian, whom we refuse to forgive for some act of unkindness, or simply because they have been more greatly blessed by God than we have been? Envy is a terrible sin, and led the religious leaders of the Jews in the days of the Lord's ministry on earth to plot His murder. Let us search our hearts about this matter, for failure to do so will embitter us, and could wreck the testimony of our local assembly.

As their punishment, the LORD announced that He would send a fire, an invading army, against both of Edom's major cities, Teman and Bozrah, and destroy them. Secular history records that Edom was conquered by the Assyrians in the eighth century BC, turned into a desolate wilderness by the fifth century BC, and overrun by the Nabateans, an Arabian tribe, between 400-300 BC. Also, several prophecies predict that the Lord Jesus will lead a campaign of final conquest against Edom when He returns in glory to earth to reign in His Millennial Kingdom; see Isaiah chapters 34 and 63. This will be the end of all anti-Semitism.

6. The LORD announces judgement on Ammon, vv. 13-15.

The fifth nation to be condemned in this catalogue of judgements is Ammon, who was related to Israel via the younger daughter of Lot, Abraham's nephew. Their crimes were terrible atrocities against Israelites in the region of Gilead, as with the Syrians earlier in the chapter, in the sole interest of enlarging their territory. It had been motivated by pure selfishness, and had led to murders of a most heinous kind, ripping open women who were pregnant, an utterly barbaric act. Both the Book of Judges and the first Book of Samuel record examples of times when the Ammonites had invaded Gilead with this motive.

Godly ambition is good, but a self-interested ambition is very destructive of others, both in the world generally, and in the lives of assemblies of the Lord's people today. As Paul says of Timothy in Philippians chapter 2 verses 20-21, 'For I have no man likeminded, who will naturally care for your state. For all seek their own, not the things which are Jesus Christ's'. That whole chapter is an antidote to selfishness, exhorting us as Christians to follow the supreme example of Christ in His path of self-humiliation to the death of the cross, and always to think of others as better, and more important, than we are. This takes a lifetime to learn and cultivate with the Lord's help. The Ammonites had not begun to learn these lessons, and the LORD judged them for their sins.

Ammon's judgement was very similar to that of the other countries, namely, invasion, destruction, and exile. Their capital city, Rabbah, which is modern Amman, the capital of Jordan, would be violently attacked and destroyed by fire amid much shouting and a strong whirlwind, evidently sent by the LORD providentially to disturb the inhabitants. The king and his princes would be included among the exiled captives. According to secular historical records, this was all fulfilled through the Assyrian conquest under Tiglath-pileser III in 734 BC. Yes, the LORD often uses the most ungodly people to execute His purposes of judgement even today. Again, we say, the LORD is sovereign over

His world, even when its inhabitants behave in the most ungodly ways. Even the wrath of man praises Him! He is the Most High, who rules in the kingdom of men, gives it to whomever He will, and sets up over it the basest of men; see Daniel 4. 17.

Amos chapter 2

1. The LORD announces judgement on Moab, vv. 1-3.

Moab's climaxing sin was the burning of the dead bones of the king of Edom into lime. This showed a revenge which did not stop even at death. This incident is not recorded specifically elsewhere in the Old Testament, but may have been perpetrated when king Jehoram of Israel and king Jehoshaphat of Judah enlisted the help of the king of Edom in a battle against the king of Moab in 2 Kings chapter 3 during the ministry of the prophet Elisha. Probably, the king of Moab was angry with the king of Edom for siding with the kings of Israel and Judah, and this was his act of vengeance executed upon him even after his death, however that may have occurred.

We should never harbour grudges against others, however unkindly they may have treated us; we should be prepared to forgive them and to forget the cause of our anger against them. In an assembly such an unforgiving spirit can quickly destroy all true fellowship. We should love our brethren self-sacrificially at all times, even when we feel that they may have wronged us, and should seek reconciliation by all means. Even if the offending brother or sister has not truly repented of their wrongdoing, we should still not let the matter breed an embittered spirit within us, but leave the issues of the wrong done with the Lord to deal with in His own time and way. He says, 'Vengeance is mine, I will repay' (Romans 12.19), and He will, often providentially.

The LORD announces the punishment of Moab to be military defeat and destruction. As with the judgement of Ammon previously, history records that this occurred when Moab was destroyed by the armies of the Assyrian king Tiglath-pileser III in 734 BC. The latter king invaded Transjordan then during one of his successful campaigns of conquest and the expansion of his empire. The palaces of Kirioth, which was one of the chief cities in Moab, otherwise known as Kerioth in Jeremiah chapter 48, or Kir of Moab in Isaiah chapter 15 verse 1, would be destroyed by fire, and the country of Moab would disappear as a nation then. Many of their citizens would be killed, including their judges and princes.

John Riddle helpfully points out that, whereas Ammon had destroyed the future by killing Israel's pregnant women, Moab had desecrated the past by exacting ultimate vengeance on their enemy, the dead king of Edom. Both victims of such outrages were helpless to resist their attackers. The LORD is the defender of the helpless, and therefore He punished both nations severely. We too should never take advantage of those who cannot defend themselves, but rather should do all we can to help them in their distress.

2. The LORD announces judgement on Judah, vv. 4-5.

It has been pointed out that, whereas the preceding Gentile nations have been condemned for sins against the laws of nature, conscience, and natural feeling, outrageous crimes against humanity, Judah and Israel are about to be condemned for persistent transgressions of the revealed will of God in the Mosaic Law given to them at Sinai. The apostle Paul, in Romans chapter 2 verse 12, outlined the principle which the LORD was following in His exercise of judgement. This verse states that, 'as many as have sinned without law', namely Damascus, Gaza, Tyre, Edom, Ammon, and Moab, 'shall also perish without law: and as many as have sinned in the law', that is Judah and Israel, 'shall be judged by law'. The LORD sets a higher standard of conduct for His own people than He does for Gentile nations, because His own people have been given more light than the Gentiles, and are therefore more responsible for their own failings than are the latter.

The citizens of the Northern Kingdom of Israel were probably not unhappy about the judgements which the LORD had just announced against many other nations, nor even very disturbed about the condemnation of their sister-nation Judah in this paragraph. However, the LORD through His servant Amos was tactfully steering His prophetic utterances gradually around to target them directly in the next paragraph and in all the following messages in the book. We are never happy when God's arrows of conviction fall on ourselves, but we should be prepared to listen to Him and to repent of the sins and shortcomings which He must always find in us as long as we are in our present bodies, and then point out to us in all faithfulness. Humility, contrition, and repentance are essential characteristics in the Christian's life, if we are ever to make progress towards true Christ-likeness.

Judah, the LORD's most favoured people, who had both the temple in their midst with His Shekinah Glory-cloud and the Davidic kingship, are here condemned for despising His law, paying no attention to it, rejecting its precepts as irrelevant to their lives, and deliberately and consistently transgressing it in many ways. They thought that they knew how to conduct their lives better than did the LORD. More than that, they had chosen to worship the false gods of the surrounding Gentile nations and to bow down to their idols. These false religions had caused them to go astray morally too. This had not been a new development either, for their fathers had been idol-worshippers even in Egypt and in the wilderness-wanderings, and had brought idols into their Promised Land from the very beginning of their occupation of it. Several Old Testament Scriptures bear witness to this sad fact.

Judah's punishment, after they had ignored many warnings and entreaties by the LORD's faithful prophets, came when Nebuchadnezzar, king of Babylon, invaded their country, besieged Jerusalem three times, and eventually, in 586 BC, sacked it and carried most of its citizens who survived the invasion into the Babylonian Exile for seventy years. Then the LORD's chosen city Jerusalem, and its glorious Temple of Solomon, would lie in ruins for many years as a warning to all who would dare to despise Him and His word.

3. *The LORD begins His condemnation and judgement of Israel, vv. 6-16.*
The LORD's arrow of conviction is now pointing firmly at the

ten tribes of Israel, the Northern Kingdom, which at this time was enjoying a period of great material prosperity and affluence. Amos does not mince his words to them. In the next three verses he condemns them for several serious sins.

First, there was legal injustice, because the judges in Israel could be bribed by the gift of money, or even a pair of sandals, to condemn those who were righteous and innocent of any charge, or simply poor.

Secondly, in verse 7a, there was oppression of the poor. It is unclear precisely what the first part of the verse means, which says that the ungodly Israelites panted 'after the dust on the head of the poor'. Perhaps they begrudged the poor the very dust that they threw on their heads as a sign of distress, or they trod the poor in the dust of the earth under their feet. They certainly perverted the just cause of the humble in court. God has always defended the poor and vulnerable from their oppressors, and so should we.

Thirdly, in verses 7b and 8, Amos exposes the people's gross immorality, which they were conducting in the name of idol worship. Both a man and his father would have intercourse with the same young woman, probably an idolatrous temple prostitute, and compound their sins by lying down beside their idol's altar on clothes which they had taken from the poor as surety for a loan that they had made to them. These heartless people used the clothes of their victims as a kind of groundsheet, on which they lay drinking wine confiscated from those they had unjustly condemned and fined. What a deplorable state the professing people of God were in at this time! It certainly called for His severe judgement.

Now, however, in verses 9 to 12, the LORD through Amos reminds His apostate people of His consistently gracious dealings with them since the day that He had redeemed them from Egypt, and then how ungratefully they had responded to this. In verse 9, He reminds them that it had been He who had destroyed the Amorite nations, that is, all the nations in Canaan, before them, despite their giants with great natural strength. Both Sihon king of Heshbon and Og, the giant king of Bashan with a huge iron bedstead, had fallen easily before the Israelite armies under Moses with the LORD's help. Before that, He had brought them triumphantly out of slavery in Egypt and led them safely through the wilderness of Sinai for forty years, in order that they might possess the Amorite's land. He had raised up some of their sons as prophets, and others as consecrated Nazarites. He knew that they understood all this, yet, sadly, they had now become as wicked and depraved as the very peoples they had dispossessed. Their wicked response had been to corrupt the LORD's Nazarites by tempting them to drink wine, which was forbidden to them under their vow, and to silence His prophets, persuading them not to communicate the LORD's messages to them.

Therefore, in verses 13-16, the LORD announces His imminent just punishment for their accumulated sins against Him. The exact meaning of verse 13 is unclear, but its general import is quite clear. The AV/KJV translation is as follows: 'Behold, I am pressed under you, as a cart is pressed that is full of sheaves', where the cart full of sheaves represents the total weight of the nation of Israel's sins upon the LORD, causing Him much grief and displeasure. However, another translation is also possible, and is represented by J.N. Darby's *New Translation*, as follows: 'Behold, I will press upon you, as a cart presseth that is full of sheaves', where the LORD is the One who will press upon the nation His punishment for all their horrendous sins. Certainly, the next verses state the punishment which would soon overtake them. No amount of speed, strength, or skill would suffice to avoid the coming punishment in the day of battle. Neither archers, nor infantry, nor cavalry would be able to save them. Even the most courageous among them would flee from the implied invading forces which would be sent against them. Amos does not here expand on the identity of these invading forces, but we shall see that they were to be the armies of the Assyrians in 722 BC, when the Northern Kingdom of Israel was overrun by them, and ceased to exist as a separate nation.

Amos chapter 3

1. Israel's great privilege as the only nation chosen by the LORD as His own earthly family means that He must punish them correspondingly more severely for their sins, vv. 1-2.

The LORD here summons the whole nation of Israel, not just the Northern Kingdom, to hear this message which He is about to reveal to Amos. A similar summons to 'hear this word' is found at the beginnings of chapters 4 and 5, and 'hear ye' also occurs at verse 13 of this present chapter. These chapters 3 to 6 form the central part of Amos's prophecy and contain the main indictments against His people, together with dire warnings of the LORD's judgements for their sins.

Because the LORD had redeemed only the nation of Israel from bondage in Egypt, had set them apart from all other nations to become His chosen earthly people, and had then brought them into covenant-relationship with Himself through both the unconditional covenants to the patriarchs, and the conditional Mosaic covenant of law at Sinai, Israel was much more responsible to respond to Him in obedience and faith than were other nations. Therefore, when they sinned, He must punish them more severely than other nations, because greater privilege always brings with it greater responsibility. This is a universal principle of judgement which God still applies today. Let us, therefore, fear to rebel against our gracious God and Father, whom we have come to trust and know in our Day of Grace, lest we too suffer His chastisement, as did ancient Israel!

2. Since every situation, including unfortunate events, has a cause, the fact that Amos has been commissioned to prophesy must mean that the LORD has a serious message to proclaim through His servant, caused by what He has seen in His people, vv. 3-8.

In these verses Amos explains why he was compelled by the LORD to prophesy at this time a message of judgement. He asks a series of seven questions which all require the answer 'No'. Every question illustrates the principle of cause and effect. There is a reason for each outcome mentioned in this passage.

In verse 3, Amos asks whether two people walk together unless they have first agreed on a specific time and place for their meeting. They have made a previous arrangement to meet, and are likeminded about it. Then, in the following verses, the questions centre around warnings of danger ignored.

In verse 4, a lion, or a young lion, only roars in the forest when he either has a prey in view, which he hopes to catch, or has already caught it. Amos was roaring prophecies of judgement against Israel because they were in danger of falling prey to their enemies, although at that precise time of prosperity in the nation this appeared to be most unlikely.

In verse 5, Amos says that a bird cannot fall victim to a trap, if there is no trap there for it to be caught by. However, if a trap does spring up, this is a sign that it has caught something. The prophet is saying that Israel stood between these two situations. There was real danger looming for them because of their sins, but the blow had not yet occurred, and Amos had been sent to warn the nation of that danger, so that they could take necessary action to avoid it.

In verse 6, the question concerning the ram's horn alarm being blown in the city warns Israel that the war-trumpet will soon be blown in their land, and cause them to fear invasion. Amos is warning his hearers that calamity can only happen to them as His people, if the LORD allows it to do so. He implies that this is certain to happen, if the nation does not listen to him.

Verse 7 assures Israel that, before the LORD does anything like this in judgement, He will reveal His secret intentions to His servants the prophets. They were Israel's watchmen, warning of danger ahead and encouraging their people's repentance.

Then, in verse 8, Amos asserts that he was compelled to preach like this against Israel's sins, because the LORD was speaking through him, warning that the lion of approaching judgement had roared, and was about to pounce upon them, and destroy them. As was the case with Jeremiah later, the LORD's message was burning like a fire within his soul, and he could not refrain from speaking it to his wayward people. Do we feel like this, when we know that we have been given a serious message to preach to the Lord's people? Certainly, we ought to.

3. The LORD through Amos again warns Israel of coming judgement by invasion for their sins, vv. 9-15.

First, in verses 9-10, the LORD through Amos summons the rulers of Israel's enemies, the Philistines represented by the city of Ashdod, and the rulers of Egypt in their palaces, to witness His condemnation of His people in Samaria for all the tumults and oppression that were regularly carried on there. Sadly, the LORD says that His people did not know how to behave righteously. The victories which the armies of Jeroboam II had won during his reign had led the Israelites to store up in their palaces the ill-gotten gains of violence and robbery. Now retribution for this unrighteous behaviour must come upon them.

In verses 11-12, the sovereign Lord GOD pronounces the sentence on the Northern Kingdom. An unnamed enemy would besiege them in their land, throw down their strongholds in which they trusted, and plunder their splendid palaces that they had built for themselves. Their military security would be suddenly destroyed. We now know that this enemy would be the Assyrians, whose kings would soon revive their policy of empire building. Only a small remnant would be rescued from the destruction, like a shepherd taking just two legs, or part of an ear, out of the mouth of a lion that has attacked his sheep. This would be all that would remain of those in Samaria who were living at ease in idle luxury in their expensive beds, or in the comfortable corners of their fine couches. The exact meaning of the end of verse 12 is unclear, but the general sense of the verse is probably similar to this paraphrastic translation. There may be a play on words with the name Damascus, which possibly was in Israelite hands at that time. According to the *Theological Wordbook of the Old Testament, Vol. 1, p. 193,* the ancient versions translated this part of the sentence as a reference to Damascus, but modern commentators usually translate it as referring to a piece, part, or corner of a couch, related to the material *damask*. We should note here that the LORD always remembers mercy when He acts in judgement, so that at least a small remnant of His people Israel will ultimately be saved to fulfil His covenant-promises to them.

Then, in verses 13-15, the sovereign, eternal, covenant-keeping Lord GOD, who is the God of all earthly and heavenly armies, the God of hosts, once again calls His hearers to witness His pronouncement of judgement on Israel, that is, particularly the Northern Kingdom here. He says that in the same day when He punishes Israel for all their transgressions He would come in judgement against their corrupt and idolatrous altars at Bethel, which Jeroboam I, the son of Nebat, had introduced to divert the people from worshipping the LORD at Jerusalem, the only true centre that He recognised. He would see that they were utterly destroyed. Not only so, but, in verse 15, the LORD states that He would destroy all the material prosperity of the people of the Northern Kingdom, including their luxurious winter and summer houses, and their expensive houses of ivory. All their great mansions would be levelled to the ground, so that there was nothing left. Such was the LORD's verdict against the apparently flourishing, but very sinful, kingdom of Jeroboam II. How like it was to many nations in the world today who have rejected the light of the Gospel of God's Grace to them! Reader, be warned, disaster lies directly ahead for such nations also!

Amos chapter 4

1. The LORD announces the sad fate of the wicked rich women of Samaria, vv. 1-3.

Once again, the LORD through Amos summons His audience to hear another message, as He had in chapter 3 verse 1. In verses 1-3, the LORD addresses the rich women of Samaria as 'cows of Bashan', which cattle were noted for being particularly well fed and strong, because Bashan contained lush pastures for them. These rich women of Samaria evidently lived in luxurious wantonness, but they only enjoyed such luxury because they oppressed the poor and needy to feed their own selfish and sinful desires for strong drink. They were obviously not submissive to their husbands, since they ordered them to bring them means of obtaining drink. This was an outrage against the LORD's holiness. Therefore, as their sovereign covenant-keeping Lord GOD, He said that their time of retribution would one day come upon them. Then He would see that they were led away into captivity with hooks in their noses or lips, every last one of them with fishhooks attached to them. Their enemies would see to it that all of them would go out straight ahead through the breaches that they had made in the city's walls, because they were being compelled to do so, and not being allowed to turn to either side in the long line of other captives.

The last phrase of verse 3 is rather obscure. It probably predicts the ultimate fate of the captured women of Samaria. The AV/KJV translation, 'and ye shall cast them into the palace', is unsatisfactory. The phrase 'into the palace' translates a Hebrew word which is found nowhere else in the Hebrew Bible, namely, '*haharmonah*'. The literal translation of this part of the sentence is, 'and you will be cast out toward Harmon'. Harmon is unidentified, but may mean Hermon, which would have been on the way to Assyria for the exiles. Others have even suggested that it means Armenia, which lay in the north of the Assyrian empire. The idea of being 'cast out' may imply that many of them would die on the forced march, and be cast out as corpses, but the exact meaning is probably now lost to us. At all events, the general import of the section is that the pleasure-loving, unfeeling rich women of Samaria, who oppressed the poor to satisfy their own fleshly and sinful desires, would be compelled to go into exile. They are a warning to us of the dangers of self-indulgence and injustice; God will judge such people very severely.

2. The LORD through Amos sarcastically encourages the Israelites to continue with their hypocritical and corrupt worship at their idolatrous shrines, because they had consistently ignored His warning chastisements designed to bring them to repentance, but then further warns them to prepare to face His very severe judgement in the near future, vv. 4-13.

The LORD speaks here with holy sarcasm. He sometimes resorts to this, in order to encourage His people to repent of their sins and to return to Him. In the Gospel records the Lord Jesus sometimes resorted to sarcasm when confronting the Jewish religious leaders, and the apostle Paul also sometimes used sarcasm in his epistles when correcting errors in the early local churches. Here the LORD tells the citizens of the Northern Kingdom to continue coming with their many and frequent sacrifices to their idolatrous calf image altars at Bethel and Gilgal, both of which places had originally been closely associated with the LORD's true dealings with Israel in the days of the conquest of the Promised Land under Joshua. When He says that they should 'multiply transgression' there, He may have meant that, as well as worshipping at the wrong centres, they would be engaging in the grossly immoral practices usually associated with these idolatrous shrines. The people were bringing their sacrifices every morning, and their tithes every three years according to the Levitical law, but their conduct contradicted their profession of devotion to the LORD. They loved to offer the appropriate sacrifices, and make great proclamations about their free will offerings, but the sovereign Lord GOD did not accept them, because their lives were not right with Him. God hates hypocrisy, and will judge us for it just like the ancient Israelites. Be warned!

Then, in verses 6-11, the LORD laments the fact that His erring people had repeatedly ignored His frequent chastisements in the form of natural calamities of various kinds. These were designed to awaken them to their sad condition and to cause them to return to Him in true repentance. He had brought famine upon them throughout their territory, and also drought conditions in some of their cities, so that some citizens had to go to other cities where rain had fallen to find water. He had stricken them with blight and mildew, and allowed locusts to destroy their vineyards, fig trees, and olive trees just when they were beginning to blossom and flourish. At other times, He had sent a plague among them similar to that with which He had plagued Egypt, or killed their young men with the sword in battle, along with their captive horses, so that their camps stank of dead corpses. Some of them He had overthrown in a way similar to that in which He had overthrown Sodom and Gomorrah, so that the few survivors were like firebrands plucked from the burning holocaust. Yet despite all these providential warning calamities, His apostate people had refused to recognise the LORD's hand of chastisement in these things, and had not repented and turned back to Him again to seek His fellowship.

Do we today recognise the voice of God in the disasters which are more and more frequently occurring in the world than they perhaps used to? Do we hear Him in these things pleading with us to repent of our sinful ways and to turn back to Him again? Are we any better than these ancient Israelites? Certainly, we must realise that the heart of man is as wicked as ever it was, and quite as set against our Maker and Redeemer as they were, but are we who read these lines hardened also?

Finally, verses 12-13 give us the LORD's sad conclusion as to the course which He must now adopt with His stubborn and hardened people Israel in the Northern Kingdom. Because they had not responded positively to any of His past judgements, He must bring upon them more severe judgements in the very near future. Therefore, the LORD challenges Israel to prepare to meet Him, their true God, in a decisive judgement. Let them remember whom they are about to face. He is the Creator of the mountains and all life, the omniscient One who can tell us our inmost thoughts, the omnipotent One who can turn morning into darkness when He wishes to, and can walk upon the high places of the earth in complete control of them. The name of the One whom they were about to meet in judgement is the LORD, the eternal, covenant-keeping God, the God who has all earthly and heavenly hosts at His bidding. Dare Israel meet Him now? How should they prepare to do so?

We today should also prepare to meet our God. We shall certainly meet Him, when the Lord Jesus Christ, who is our great God and Saviour, returns to this sad world again, first to rapture all true Christians to glory with Him, where they will be reviewed at His august Judgement Seat, then to the earth again to reign over the world for a thousand years in peace and righteousness. If we have not previously trusted Christ, the Judge of all men, during our lives on earth, we must still face Him, our Creator, would-be Redeemer, and Judge, in eternity at the Great White Throne judgement, where He will decide on the degree of our eternal punishment in the Lake of Fire. Either way, we shall one day meet Him, and receive His verdict on our lives. Reader, have you yet met Christ as your Saviour and bowed your knees to Him as your Lord? That is the only right way in which we can prepare to meet our God during the Age of Grace. In eternity it will be too late to prepare. Be warned, and be reconciled to God in Christ today!

Amos chapter 5

1. The LORD through Amos laments for His fallen people Israel, and pleads with them to repent and seek Him again before the coming judgement destroys them, vv. 1-9.

Chapters 5 and 6 form the third and last sermon which Amos preached to the Northern Kingdom of Israel in the centre section of his prophecy. It begins in the same way as did the two previous sermons in chapters 3 and 4, as the LORD through Amos summons Israel to 'hear this word' against them. Here, as there, there is first an indictment for their sins, then, from verse 16 onwards, a declaration of the coming imminent judgement for these sins intermingled with further calls to repentance and transformed behaviour. The LORD always leaves the way open for restoration, until it is clear that there will be no repentance and our hearts are completely hardened against His loving pleas to us.

In verses 1-3, the LORD takes up a sorrowful lament for Israel, for He sees her as a fallen virgin whom none can raise up again to a life of rectitude and purity, and who is about to be forsaken in her land, forlorn and hopeless before her enemies who will soon attack her. In verse 3, He says, as the sovereign, covenant-keeping Lord GOD of Israel that, after the coming invasion, only a tenth of the total population of the Northern Kingdom will survive. He refers to the Assyrian invasion, which took place not many years after Amos preached this series of sermons. At the time when he wrote his prophecy this seemed to be a very remote possibility, since the Northern Kingdom was then enjoying a period of affluence and success in battle, but appearances are deceptive, and the LORD can easily alter the fortunes of kingdoms very quickly. Our God is always in absolute control of the world situation, and our individual lives also. We today should heed this warning urgently, and turn to God again to seek His forgiveness for our nation's sins and learn to live differently.

In fact, in verses 4-9, the LORD now pleads with His people through His faithful servant to seek Him, so that they might live and not suffer the fate of which He had warned them. Let them not seek the corrupt and idolatrous calf worship at Bethel, Gilgal, and Beersheba, because no help would come to them from these false shrines. Gilgal would be destroyed in the coming captivity, and Bethel would come to nothing also. Rather, let them seek Him, the LORD, their true, eternal, faithful, covenant-keeping God, and then they would live, for otherwise He was about to destroy them like a consuming fire, and their counterfeit idolatrous image at Bethel would certainly not be able to prevent this disaster overtaking them. He reminded them that they were descended from Joseph, who was true to the LORD throughout his life and eventually blessed for this, but He implied that they could not depend on their family connections for deliverance; they must themselves repent and trust their God, as is true of us today also. In verse 7, Amos reminded the people that they were guilty of perverting justice and abandoning righteousness in their dealings with one another, so that their application of the law had become as bitter and poisonous to their citizens as wormwood. It is so sad when we cannot trust the lawyers among us to deliver righteous verdicts in our courts.

In verse 8, he reminded them also of the absolute greatness of the LORD, their covenant-God, for He alone is the One who has created the constellations of stars such as the Pleiades (AV 'the seven stars') and Orion. He is easily able to turn the deep darkness of death into the morning, and the day into night again, as He does every twenty-four hour day. He also controls the waters of the sea, and causes them to flood over the earth when He wishes. Yes, the LORD is His name, eternal, omnipotent, and Israel's God also. Let His erring people seek Him, and the catastrophe could be averted. Otherwise, He warns them that He is quite capable of flashing forth destruction upon the nation's strongholds, so that ruin overtakes all their fortresses, which they thought to be quite impregnable. Their only hope was to seek the LORD in true repentance, and thus avoid His judgement. It is our only hope too. Reader, be warned!

2. *The LORD through Amos further reminds Israel of all their many sins of injustice and oppression of the poor among them, but again urges them to repent of their ways and to begin to practise good instead, since then He might be gracious to them as the descendants of Joseph, vv. 10-15.*

In verses 10-12, the LORD accuses the people of Israel of many blatant sins of which He knew that they were guilty. First, they hated honest judges who delivered righteous verdicts and rebukes in their administration of justice in the lawcourts at the gates of the cities; in fact, they shunned all who did speak uprightly, so corrupt were they. The moral fibre of the nation had perished. Because the rich trampled on the poor, and extorted from them unjust taxes of wheat, their basic food, the LORD would see to it that they would never enjoy living in the fine houses that they had built for themselves of hewn stone, nor enjoy drinking wine from the desirable vineyards that they had planted. He knew all about their many and various sins of injustice and bribery in court to secure an unjust verdict against the poor. For that reason, those who were still prudent in the nation thought it best to keep quiet about all these abuses, since the Northern Kingdom of Israel was then a very evil environment for anyone to live in.

However, once again, the LORD through Amos pleaded with the people to seek to do good, not evil, so that they might avert the coming danger and live. Then He, the LORD God of hosts, the eternal God who controls all situations in the world, would truly be with them, as they fondly, but mistakenly, were imagining because of their empty ritual worship at the idolatrous altars. To really secure His favour and avoid the tragedy of exile they must hate evil and love what was good; they must establish true justice in their lawcourts. Then, perhaps, after all, it was not too late to be delivered from their enemies. We should notice here how frequently the LORD opened the way back to Himself for Israel to repent and live. He does not ever afflict mankind willingly, only when all other options open to Him have been exhausted, and His holiness demands just retribution. God does the same with us today. Have we all responded to Him in repentant faith and grateful obedience?

3. The LORD announced Israel's punishment in the coming Day of the LORD, when He would cause them to be exiled by the Assyrians beyond Damascus, vv. 16-27.

From this point in the sermon onwards until the end of chapter 6 the LORD through Amos announces Israel's appropriate punishment for all their sins, with little further encouragement to repentance. His people in the Northern Kingdom had frustrated His patience, and judgement must fall on them decisively.

First, therefore, in verses 16-17, the LORD in His capacity as Israel's covenant-God, sovereign, and in control of all powers in heaven and earth, predicted that there would be wailing in all the streets and highways of the Northern Kingdom, as the surviving people, including all the farmers, mourned for those who had been killed, using professional mourners. There would be mourning in all the vineyards, which were normally the source of joy to the people, as the LORD passed through the land in judgement, just as He had once done in Egypt at the Exodus.

Then, in verses 18-20, the LORD pronounced a devastating woe on those of His people who wanted the prophesied Day of the LORD to come, since they imagined that it would bring them hope and deliverance, victory over their enemies and blessing. He asked what good it would be to them, and declared that it would rather be a time of darkness and judgement for them, not light and blessing at all. It would be a time when anyone who tried to escape from one dreadful danger would find themselves suddenly facing another even greater danger. No, the ultimate Day of the LORD will certainly be the time when the LORD puts this sad world right, but it will first involve severe judgement for rebellious mankind, before He establishes the Millennial Kingdom of Christ with all its accompanying blessings and light. In actual fact, the Northern Kingdom of Israel was about to face a time of judgement which would foreshadow the final Day of the LORD, but would not be the ultimate fulfilment of these prophecies.

We know today from other Scriptures that the only way to avert these coming catastrophes is to repent and believe the Gospel of God's Grace before the Day of Grace ends, and Christ returns to the air to rapture His redeemed Church to heaven. Only New Testament Church believers have been promised that they will never face God's wrath, but be delivered from the whole time when He does pour out His righteous wrath on this rebellious world. The Israelites, like all mankind today, needed to learn that, if God were to intervene in this world now during the Day of Grace, it would have to be in judgement, and they would become the deserving objects of His wrath just as much as will all other unbelievers. No, the longsuffering silence of the LORD during the present time is designed to give all of us the opportunity to repent, believe the gospel, and go on to live changed lives that please God, see 2 Peter chapter 3. Now is the day of salvation, and not judgement. Praise His Name!

4. Now the LORD declares that He finds Israel's hypocritical religious ritual repugnant, and tells His people rather to cease their ritual and to begin to practise righteous behaviour instead, vv. 21-24.

Religious activity without heart reality is always an abomination to God. This even applies to what were originally divinely-ordained forms of worship and insincere expressions of devotion. He finds empty formalism nauseating, and this angers Him rather than pleases Him. We today need to search our hearts to see if we are guilty of hypocritical worship even when we are professing to follow divinely given commands in Scripture, such as at the weekly Lord's Supper. Because His people's lives were not right, He hated and despised their feast days and solemn assemblies, nor would He accept their offerings, although they might be offering them according to the Levitical law. He did not want their noisy, but insincere, songs, sung to the melody of stringed instruments. Instead, He called for them to let their everyday lives be bathed in justice and acts of righteousness.

Here J.A. Motyer points out that this verse contains a Hebrew pun, or play on words, in the phrase (literally translated), 'let justice roll down like waters'. The word for 'roll', which is from the verb root *galal*, reminds us of the name Gilgal, where the Israelites' reproach of Egypt was rolled away after they had been circumcised in the time of Joshua before the conquest of the Promised Land. However, at the time when Amos was writing it was one of the chief centres of the Northern Kingdom's idolatry. So here the LORD is saying, 'Yes, you have been to Gilgal, but there is a rolling you have forgotten, the rolling of justice and righteousness'. He did not want hypocritical ritual, but was looking for completely transformed lives. This is what really pleases Him today also. We need to search our hearts to see whether, or not, *we* are giving Him His true desire.

5. The LORD challenges Israel to consider their blatant idolatry, which was practised even during the wilderness-wanderings, and then announces that, because of this apostasy, He is now going to cause them to be carried away into exile beyond Damascus by the Assyrians, vv. 25-27.

Verse 25 has caused many commentators some difficulty, since it appears to suggest that the Israelites did not offer sacrifices to the LORD during their wilderness-wanderings for forty years. According to the Pentateuch, this is clearly not the case, since the record there often states that they did offer many sacrifices to the LORD then. Probably, the answer to the difficulty is that, although many of them did go through the motions of offering sacrifices to the LORD then, as they were commanded to do, their hearts were not in this service, because, as the following verse says, they were at the same time continuing to engage in idolatrous worship, which they had learned to practise in Egypt and had never completely given up.

John Riddle suggests that the verse should be understood like this, 'Yes, you did bring sacrifices and offerings in the wilderness, but you did not bring them *unto Me*'. There was even then no reality about their worship of the LORD, just as there was no reality about it in the days of Amos, for they were living a double life, pretending to worship the LORD, but also worshipping their various idols, which they were carrying with them all through the wilderness days. The translation of verse 26 is somewhat difficult, but it clearly refers to the names of some of the pagan idols which

Concise Commentary on Amos chapter 5

the Israelites were worshipping during the wilderness wanderings. The AV/KJV translates it, 'But ye have borne the tabernacle of your Moloch and Chiun your images, the star of your god, which ye made to yourselves.' The NASB translates the verse as follows, 'You also carried along Sikkuth your king and Kiyyun, your images, the star of your gods which you made for yourselves.' In Joshua chapter 24, Joshua tells the first generation of Israelites who entered the Promised Land to put away their false gods, which their fathers served beyond the River Euphrates and in Egypt, and to worship and serve the LORD alone and wholeheartedly. This clearly implies that at least some of the people then were still harbouring idols which they worshipped. We know that many of them worshipped the golden calf at the foot of Mount Sinai, and, in his defence before the Jewish Sanhedrin in Acts chapter 7 verses 41-43, Stephen said that this was the beginning of a downward course which led to complete apostasy and idolatry in the nation later in the days of Amos. There was, therefore, probably at least some idol worship amongst the Israelites during the wilderness days and even during the conquest of the land, although some commentators do disagree with this statement.

It was not without good reason that the apostle John at the end of his first letter warns true believers to 'keep, or guard, yourselves from idols', 1 John 5. 21. Anyone, or anything, that takes the place in our hearts and lives of the LORD Himself is an idol, and must be utterly rejected. Even when we are appearing to worship the LORD, we may be just going through the motions hypocritically. This is completely unacceptable to God, who is the Only True God and has done everything to save us. Are we today really sincere in our worship of the Lord? Have we any idols? Are we secretly living a double life? If so, we need to repent, or we will face the Lord's severe chastisement.

Then, in verse 27, the LORD announces the inevitable judgement for this apostasy, exile beyond Damascus: that is, by the Assyrians in their land, although the Assyrians are not actually specifically named in any part of the Book of Amos. As J.A. Motyer says, 'The gods of Assyria occupied the hearts of Israel long before the armies of Assyria occupied its streets and towns... "the LORD, whose name is The God of hosts" will not be mocked'. Some of the gods mentioned above were gods worshipped by the Assyrians. In his quotation in Acts chapter 7, Stephen said that the Israelites would be exiled 'beyond Babylon', rather than Damascus, because he anticipated the final destination of all the remaining Israelites later in the days of Nebuchadnezzar in 586 BC. The whole nation of Israel was about to collapse in exile in their enemies' land. That was their deserved fate for their sins. We today should also be warned not to depart from the LORD our God! That is the surest way to spiritual ruin and disaster.

Amos chapter 6

1. The LORD through Amos pronounces a woe on the idle rich ruling classes in both Jerusalem and Samaria, who mistakenly thought that their kingdoms were better than those of the surrounding Gentile nations, vv. 1-6.

In chapter 5 verse 18, Amos had pronounced a woe on those who wanted the Day of the LORD to come soon, because they mistakenly imagined that it would be a time of victory and blessing for their kingdom. Now, in this chapter, he pronounced another devastating woe on the indolent wealthy ruling classes in both the kingdom of Judah and the Northern Kingdom of Israel. Here Judah is included in the LORD's condemnation, because, sadly, its leaders were no better than the leaders of the Northern Kingdom. Although the Southern Kingdom did have some better kings in the Davidic dynasty, and for a time followed the LORD somewhat more closely than did the Northern Kingdom, eventually it sank to the same depths of apostasy and moral degeneracy as did their neighbour, and failed to learn anything from the catastrophe which was about to befall Samaria. Mankind have always failed to learn much from the salutary lessons which history could teach us all, because we are all by nature incorrigible, apart from the grace of God.

In order to understand the full meaning of verse 1, it is advisable to read it in a more recent translation, such as the NASB, as follows, 'Woe to those who are at ease in Zion, and to those who feel secure in the mountain of Samaria, the distinguished men of the foremost of nations, to whom the house of Israel comes'. The rich leaders of Judah were complacent about their easy circumstances in the stronghold of Zion, thinking that they were quite safe from attack. Likewise, the leaders in the Northern Kingdom felt quite secure in their mountain citadel in Samaria. They were proud and self-satisfied, flattered that the citizens of Israel's two kingdoms used to come to them for help and guidance. The LORD hates a proud look, and an attitude of superiority in us, since we have nothing that He did not first give us, and we are all by nature helpless sinners in need of His grace. The long and successful reigns of both Uzziah in Judah and Jeroboam II in Israel had created in them, not a sense of humble gratitude for easier circumstances, but a false sense of security and superiority to others.

Verse 2 can be understood in one of two different ways. The divided kingdoms of Israel are encouraged to compare themselves with some of the great Gentile cities around them, such as Calneh in Assyria on the River Tigris, Hamath the great city in Syria, and Gath in the land of the Philistines, and to consider whether, or not, these other cities were better than their own kingdoms, or had a wider territory than they had at that time. If the answer to these questions is 'No', then Amos is saying that these other cities are not worthy to be compared with Israel's kingdoms; Israel is the best of all. However, the context may suggest that the answer expected to these questions is probably 'Yes', that these Gentile cities are actually better in many ways than Israel is at this time, both morally and spiritually. It is very sad when the character and conduct of the LORD's own people are worse than those of our unsaved neighbours. It invites His severe chastisement. Pride always goes before a fall!

Verse 3 indicates that the leaders of Israel were quite deluded in their thinking that the evil day of calamity was far away from them in the future; in fact, it was being brought much nearer by their careless and degenerate conduct. The day of reckoning was fast approaching, when they would be subjected to what is here called 'the seat of violence', probably meaning a reign of terror by their enemies over them in the captivities, both in Assyria for the Northern Kingdom, and later in Babylon for Judah.

In verses 4-6, before Amos spells out the LORD's sentence of captivity on them in verse 7, he describes the contemporary degenerate lifestyle of the nation's leaders in some detail with obvious disgust. They were completely self-indulgent. In their laziness they reclined on expensive beds of ivory, and sprawled on their fine couches, eating choice lambs from the flock and calves from the best of the herd. Their pointless hobby was improvising music to the sound of the harp, and they had composed songs for themselves like David, but without any of his spiritual character. They drank wine from sacrificial bowls, thus desecrating them, while, to complete their culture of the body, they anointed themselves with the finest of oils. Their lives were thoroughly self-centred, and they had not grieved at all for those in their kingdom who were suffering affliction through poverty or outright injustice, nor did they anticipate the imminent national ruin of Israel's ten northern tribes, which had once contained spiritual men like Joseph. They were totally blind to their sad spiritual and moral condition, and oblivious to the great danger in which they stood, as is often the case with those who have departed from the LORD.

Christians today need to beware of succumbing to the prevailing apathy, secularism, and self-centred materialism of our contemporary world, especially in the western nations, which once valued spiritual things much more than they do now. We should value honest work and self-disciplined behaviour like our forebears who communicated the gospel to us in past years. To reject this latter wholesome lifestyle is a road to disaster, both individually and nationally.

2. The sovereign Lord GOD swore by Himself that, because of their licentious behaviour and unjust rule, and in spite of their obnoxious arrogance about their recent military successes, these men would be the first to go into exile at the hands of an invading nation, the Assyrians, and very few of their citizens would survive, vv. 7-16.

In verse 7, the LORD pronounced their sentence once again; the indolent and corrupt rulers would very soon go into exile, leading the sad procession of prisoners trailing behind them. This would bring a sudden end to the sprawlers' banqueting, a rude awakening to the reality of their situation. 'Eat, drink, and be merry, for tomorrow we die', is a very foolish philosophy of life to follow. Now they would have to face the wrath of their covenant-

Lord GOD, the almighty LORD God of hosts, who says in verse 8 that, because He hated the pride of His wayward people Israel in the ten northern tribes, and detested their military citadels, because they trusted more in them than in Himself, He was going to deliver up the city of Samaria and everything it contained to their enemies for complete destruction.

Verses 9-11 present to us a very tragic scene of death in the houses of the Northern Kingdom in the aftermath of the nation's fall to the Assyrians following the long siege of Samaria. Ten surviving men in one house would all die, and then a close relative, or an undertaker, would carry the last dead body out, probably for cremation to avoid infection spreading. If there was any survivor in the innermost parts of the house, they would be asked, 'Is anyone else with you?' The answer would be, 'No one'. Then he would be told, 'Keep quiet, for the name of the LORD is not to be mentioned'. Even the few survivors would refuse to acknowledge the name of the LORD, who had caused the tragedy to happen. So far was the nation from God that they would try to blot out all memory of Him who was their covenant-LORD God. Unbelieving men and women today try to do the same thing when a tragedy strikes which is obviously an act of God. They refuse to acknowledge Him, or to turn to Him in repentance, for that hurts their pride. In verse 11, the LORD confirms that He is going to command that both the great mansions of Israel and the smaller houses in the country should be smashed to smithereens.

Then, in verses 12-14, the LORD through Amos points out to his hearers the absurdity of their wicked behaviour, which had precipitated the imminent disaster in the nation. It is both ridiculous and dangerous to make horses run on rocks, or to plough them with oxen, because the animals will become seriously injured. The RSV emends the text of the second line of this half of verse 12, to read, 'plough the sea with oxen', another absurd venture which is impossible, and would lead to disaster. However, the usual Hebrew vocalisation of the line is quite satisfactory, and gives the same basic sense. Then Amos says that the people of Israel had done something just as stupid and dangerous, namely, they had turned justice into gall, or poison, and 'the fruit of righteousness into hemlock', that is, they had perverted justice in their lawcourts, victimising the poor and acquitting the guilty. Such unjust behaviour was sure to rebound upon them, and bring them into trouble, both individually and nationally. There is an inevitable moral law in the world of sowing and reaping exactly what we sow, whether good or bad. The LORD's people had ignored this, and were about to suffer the consequences for their immorality and injustice.

Furthermore, the LORD reminded them that they were taking all the credit for their recent national military successes under Jeroboam II to themselves, and ignoring His part in helping them win a few victories. On the contrary, the inspired historian of Israel's history in 2 Kings chapter 14 verses 23-29 records that it was the LORD who had, through Jonah, predicted victory for them, after He had seen the affliction of Israel, and had 'saved them by the hand of Jeroboam the son of Joash'. God had helped their armies to win back territory lost in previous years, but now He was being ignored. Mankind are always prone to attribute all their successes to their own prowess, but to blame God for all their afflictions and defeats. How conceited we so often are and ungrateful, when actually we owe everything to God anyway! In verse 13, there may be a reference to two minor towns which Jeroboam had captured. 'A thing of nought' may refer to a place called Lo-debar, and the 'horns' may be a reference to a place called Karnaim, which means 'two horns', but this reference is not certain.

Finally in this third major sermon, in verse 14, the LORD, the God of hosts, all armies, both earthly and heavenly, declares clearly His intention to raise up a nation against the Northern Kingdom, namely, the Assyrians, who would afflict Israel throughout their country, from the entrance of Hemath, or Hamath, in the north beside Syria, to the river of the wilderness, that is, to the Kidron by the Jordan in the valley of the Arabah in the south. Nothing would be allowed to escape from their invading forces. Israel had 'sown the wind', and would now 'reap the whirlwind', as Hosea, Amos' fellow-prophet to the Northern Kingdom, predicted about the same time as did Amos, see Hosea 8. 7.

Amos chapter 7

Now the LORD begins to further warn Israel concerning their imminent judgement through a sequence of five vivid visions which He gave to Amos. This sequence is interrupted briefly in chapter 7 verses 10-17 by an interesting and instructive historical confrontation between Amos and the false priest of Bethel at the time, a man called Amaziah. Then the sequence of visions is resumed in chapters 8 and 9.

1. The LORD's first vision to Amos of grasshoppers, or locusts, attacking the land of Israel at the beginning of the people's harvest time, vv. 1-3.

Amos here reports to the people of the Northern Kingdom the first threatening vision which the nation's sovereign, covenant-keeping Lord GOD had shown him. The LORD was forming a swarm of grasshoppers, probably a kind of locust, to destroy the latter growth of the harvest in spring time. Since the first crop of the harvest was demanded by the king as his tax from the common people, known here as 'the king's mowings', the latter depended for their livelihood entirely on the second crop. If for any reason that failed, then they would be destitute of food. That was the dire situation depicted in the LORD's vision to Amos. Locust plagues were one of the means by which the LORD disciplined His wayward people, according to Deuteronomy chapter 28 verse 38.

In his vision, Amos saw that the locust swarm had finished eating all the vegetation of the land, so that there was nothing left. Then, seeing this, Amos began to intercede in prayer for the people of Israel, pleading that the LORD would pardon them, on the ground that they could not withstand this judgement and

Concise Commentary on Amos chapter 7

would be entirely destroyed, because they were really very small and weak. We see here that Amos did have a more sympathetic side to his character; he was moved by the imminent plight of his beloved people, whom he calls Jacob, reminding the LORD of Israel's sinful old nature. The LORD responded at once to His servant's fervent plea by relenting of His purpose, and telling Amos that He would not yet destroy Israel. Other faithful servants of the LORD, such as Moses and Samuel, had interceded for Israel when they were about to face severe chastisement or summary judgement for their sins, and had been heeded by Him. We should confess our faults to one another, and pray for one another, that we may be healed of the ills with which the LORD has inflicted us for our sins, James 5. 16. Thus far, therefore, Amos secured a delay of execution for the Northern Kingdom by his godly intervention on their behalf. He did not really want them to suffer.

2. The LORD's second vision to Amos of a consuming fire, and the prevailing intercessory prayer of Amos for Israel, to which again the LORD gave heed, and decided not to judge His people yet, vv. 4-6.

In his second vision from the LORD, Amos saw a consuming fire sent to contend with Israel. It completely destroyed the great reservoir of water beneath the earth, and began to destroy their farming territory also. When Amos saw the great danger that Israel was in, he again pleaded with the LORD, although he knew that He was the absolutely sovereign Lord GOD, to halt the judgement, lest Israel in their weakness should be completely destroyed, and the unconditional promises made to the nation's forefathers fail to be fulfilled. God can be reasoned with, if our prayers affect, defend, and promote His name and glory in the world. At times, He also reasons with us about our foolish sins, because He does not really want to punish us for them, but to bless us instead. Here, therefore, He listened to His faithful servant Amos, and relented of the further judgement which He was threatening to bring upon Israel. The LORD really hoped that Israel would repent, so that He need not punish them at all. That is why He gave the nation two more opportunities to avoid the judgements which Amos saw so vividly in his first two visions.

3. In the LORD's third vision to Amos of a plumb-line measuring a vertical wall, in order to test whether it was truly perpendicular, He said that, having tested His people Israel, and found them completely defective, He would now no longer spare them, but would destroy both the pagan sanctuaries in the country and the dynasty of Jeroboam II with the sword, vv. 7-9.

The LORD's great longsuffering with His wayward and unrepentant people could not last forever, for He must ultimately act in accordance with His absolute holiness and the demands of His great name and glory. After a first and then a second stay of execution, summary judgement must fall on them. Similar opportunities are to be given to heretics associated with New Testament assemblies to repent, before they are rejected finally for their sins. 'A man that is an heretic after the first and second admonition reject'; Titus 3. 10. God is slow to anger and has great mercy. How thankful we are of that truth about His character! However, let us never presume on His mercy and grace, but repent speedily whenever we are aware that we have sinned against Him, for there are necessary limits to the exercise of His longsuffering with all of us. Reader, be warned!

In his vision, Amos saw the sovereign Lord, *Adonai*, standing on a wall made with a plumb-line, holding a plumb-line in His hand to test whether, or not, the wall had been made correctly perpendicular. He told Amos that He would put the plumb-line against His people Israel, and that, if He found that their behaviour was quite unrighteous, He would not overlook them again in His judgement, but punish them severely. Evidently, He had already found that they had strayed far from His righteous standards, because He immediately announced their punishment. He was about to destroy all their idolatrous pagan altars, which are here, unusually, called 'the high places of Isaac'. Compare verse 16 of this chapter, where the nation is called 'the house of Isaac'. These are the only references in the Old Testament where Isaac represents the whole nation, rather than Abraham, Israel, or Jacob. We do not now know why this is so, but perhaps at this time in their history the northern tribes particularly revered Isaac. They were evidently using his name in connection with their idolatrous worship. The LORD also decreed that the other pagan sanctuaries of Israel would be laid waste, and that the house, or dynasty, of Jeroboam II would be finally destroyed by the sword. This occurred not long after Amos prophesied this. Zechariah, the son of Jeroboam II, was assassinated after a very short reign of six months, and the northern tribes then had a succession of five further kings who reigned for only quite short periods, and were largely brought to power by violent coups and assassinations. The Northern Kingdom became very unstable before it was overwhelmed by the Assyrians in 722 BC, and its citizens carried into exile.

Thus the LORD's prophecy by Amos was fulfilled to the letter in the near future from the time that Amos declared it, although at the time Jeroboam II seemed to be very firmly established in his kingdom, leading an affluent and successful society. Reader, we today should be warned not to despise and refuse to believe the LORD's predictions concerning Christ's approaching second coming just because at present it seems unlikely to happen. Christ will come again, just as surely and literally as He did the first time. Are we all ready to meet Him then?

4. Amos, when he is accused of treason by Amaziah, King Jeroboam's false priest at Bethel, and ordered to stop prophesying, tells Amaziah his own credentials as a true prophet of the LORD, and proceeds to denounce Amaziah, predicting his exile and death, vv. 10-17.

False religionists frequently oppose and accuse the faithful servants of God when they preach the truth of Scripture to them and their congregations, because the truth hurts their pride and reveals their sinful and selfish ways. It was so in the days of the Lord Jesus' ministry, when the Jewish religious leaders attacked Him and sought to discredit Him. Pilate knew that it was on account of envy that they had brought Christ to him for execution, Matthew 27. 18. Amos and all the prophets of the LORD in the Old Testament found this attitude no different in their days.

Amaziah, the false priest of Bethel, where Jeroboam the son of Nebat had originally set up his idolatrous calf-image as the shrine to which all the ten northern tribes were meant to come to worship, instead of going to the LORD's true centre at the temple in Jerusalem, took violent exception to Amos' dire prediction of the imminent destruction of the dynasty of Jeroboam II, the contemporary king of Israel, by the sword of an invader, and the captivity of the Northern Kingdom in a foreign land. He sent an urgent message to Jeroboam II, saying that Amos had conspired against him and his nation, and thus had committed treason. Amaziah implied that the country could no longer endure all Amos' prophetic utterances, and so the offensive prophet should be banished. At the same time, the false cleric confronted Amos in Bethel directly, probably fearing that he was a rival to his authority in the Northern Kingdom, and told him to flee from Israel back to Judah, and only to prophesy there. At all events, so he said, let Amos not prophesy again at Bethel, since it was, in Amaziah's words, 'the king's chapel', or sanctuary, and 'the king's court', or royal palace, reserved for him and his idolatrous priests alone. Amaziah's description of Amos in verse 12 as 'thou seer' may be a derogatory reference to his prophetic ministry, since it possibly implies that Amos was just a visionary out of touch with the realities of life in the Northern Kingdom.

However, the grandiose descriptions of the altar at Bethel as 'the king's chapel' and 'the king's court' suggest the presence of an obnoxious ecclesiastical pretension and great spiritual pride, and they surely have some telling parallels with the sad situation in our own beloved country of the United Kingdom. Here the great cathedral of Canterbury and other similar imposing architectural structures throughout the land are mistakenly called 'houses of God', reserved primarily for the benefit of our reigning monarchs and the clergy, and thought to be especially holy places where the LORD dwells more truly than in the hearts of His believing people. Our respected king or queen can never truly be described as 'the head of the Church of England', since Christ is the only true Head of the Church dispensational, and He is in heaven today. Nor does the LORD now dwell in church buildings made with hands; the latter are simply convenient structures built to facilitate the worship and service of His believing people who usually meet in them.

Concise Commentary on Amos chapter 7

In verses 14-15, Amos rises to this challenge from the idolatrous priest, and gives Amaziah a telling account of his humble background and genuine call to serve the LORD as His prophet to Israel. He was telling Amaziah that, although he was an uneducated man from the working and farming classes, the LORD had genuinely called him to his present task as a faithful prophet, which, he implied, was more than could be said for Amaziah and all his idolatrous priests at Bethel. We should not despise or ignore uneducated servants of the LORD today, but honour those who are deeply taught in the Scriptures and living close to their Master in heaven with a genuine call and commission to preach to others the messages which He has clearly given them. It is not necessary to have a theology degree before we can preach the Scriptures effectively. Believing scholarship is a good tool of study, but a very bad master. The latter situation creates an unofficial clergy amongst the saints, but we are really all members one of another in the fellowship of any local assembly, using our God-given gifts to help our fellow-believers to grow more like Christ and to serve Him better.

Amos here frankly confesses that he was not a prophet originally, perhaps meaning that he did not attend one of the schools of prophets, nor was he the son of a prophet, with a good family background. No, he had been a herdsman, a kind of shepherd, or sheepmaster, of dwarf sheep, and also a gatherer, farmer, or tender, of sycamore fruit and trees, which were quite lowly occupations. Then he recounted his call by the LORD as he was following his flock, busily engaged in his rightful duties. The LORD simply told him to go and prophesy to His people Israel, in the Northern Kingdom primarily, but also in the Southern Kingdom of Judah, where he had lived before. So often servants of the Lord are called from the midst of busy occupations to preach or serve Him in some other way; God does not usually call lazy believers. There is a saying in ordinary life, that, if you want a job done well, give it to someone who is already very busy, and he will be able to do it better than anyone else. Self-discipline is a great virtue.

Now, therefore, in verses 16-17, having stated his credentials as a true prophet of the LORD to all Israel, Amos delivered a withering rebuff to the false cleric Amaziah. He had a special message from the LORD for him. Amos then said that, although Amaziah had forbidden him to prophesy against Israel, probably here meaning the Northern Kingdom, nor to continue spouting messages of judgement against 'the house of Isaac', who may have been especially honoured in the pagan rituals of the ten northern tribes at that time, he had a dire warning for him. His wife would become a prostitute in the city, his sons and daughters would be killed by the sword of the coming invader, his territory would be divided up with a survey-line by others, and he himself would die in an unclean foreign land, while Israel would certainly soon go into captivity away from their own land. As elsewhere in this prophecy, the captors expected to execute this sad prediction are understood to be the Assyrians, who would overrun the nation in 722 BC after a long siege of Samaria. The latter are never named throughout the book, but their identity is certain when other historical sources, Biblical and secular, are compared with this prophecy.

Amos chapter 8

1. The LORD shows Amos His fourth vision, of a basket of summer fruit, and explains its significance, vv. 1-3.

Now in another vivid vision, the sovereign Lord GOD showed Amos a basket of summer fruit, and specially directed his attention to it, in order that he might understand what the LORD was telling him by it. Evidently, the fruit was ripe to be eaten. The LORD explained the significance of the illustration, saying that the end had come for His people Israel, by whom He then especially meant the Northern Kingdom. Israel was ripe for judgement to fall upon them imminently. Here we need to understand that the passage in the original language contains an instructive Hebrew play on two similar words, a pun, namely, *qayits,* which means 'summer fruit', and *qets,* which means 'end'. In this sequence of visions, the judgement of God on Israel becomes ever more imminent and urgent. The LORD said that He would not pass by them again in longsuffering mercy, but must now vindicate His name and holy character. The usual songs of joy and praise which normally accompanied the harvest home in the temple would become sad wailings in that day of judgement and destruction. By 'the temple' He probably means here the Northern Kingdom's counterfeit temple, perhaps the one at Bethel, introduced by the first Jeroboam, the son of Nebat, in order to divert his people from the true temple of Solomon in Jerusalem, lest they return their allegiance back to the dynasty of David. In the day of judgement there would be many dead bodies strewn everywhere, and these would be cast out unceremoniously for disposal in complete silence, without any official mourning ritual as a mark of respect for those who had died. It would be a ghastly and hopeless scene, caused entirely by the persistent sins of the LORD's apostate professing people, some of which He proceeds to describe again, as He did earlier in the book.

2. Having spelled out some examples of Israel's gross injustice against the poor, the LORD declares His determination to judge the pride of His professing people in a series of horrific 'acts of God', followed by a prediction that there would one day be a spiritual famine in the land, so that no-one would be able to find the true word of the LORD to them, and the Northern Kingdom's false religion would be unable to satisfy their spiritual thirst, vv. 4-14.

The LORD addresses those in the nation of Israel who trampled on the poor, and did away with humble people in the land by dishonest commercial trading as soon as the new moon and Sabbath celebrations were over. How hypocritical they were to be religiously keeping these feasts, but then exploiting their neighbours as soon as they could! They falsified the correct weights and measures, and used dishonest scales, in order to buy the helpless for money, the needy for a mere pair of sandals, and to sell even the worst of the wheat. God hates such selfish acts of injustice, and proceeds to announce His severe judgements for them.

Therefore, in verses 7-10, the LORD declares that, because He hates the arrogant pride of His unrepentant professing people Jacob and would never forget any of their wicked deeds, He is about to judge them with many cataclysmic 'acts of God'. Because of these gross injustices He would cause the land to be shaken by earthquakes which would bring death and destruction to everyone who dwelt in it. Significantly, Amos dates his prophecy 'two years before the earthquake' in chapter 1 verse 1, and we noted there that that earthquake must have been a very severe one, since it is mentioned again by Zechariah in the sixth century BC, in Zechariah chapter 14 verse 5, many years later than the eighth century BC, when Amos was writing. Then the end of verse 8 seems to be predicting a tsunami, an earthquake under the sea, which causes the waters on the surface of the earth to rise above their normal level. The heaving of the earth's tectonic plates is likened to the flooding of the Nile in Egypt annually, and its subsiding again after the inundation. Also, there would, at the same time, be an eclipse of the sun at midday, which would cause the earth to be shrouded in darkness. Such things used to cause the ancient peoples great fear. F.A. Tatford records that there was

Concise Commentary on Amos chapter 8

just such an eclipse of the sun in Israel on 15th June, 763 BC, which therefore may have been the time of the fulfilment of this prophecy. In Scripture, the darkening of the sun is likened to the judgement of God, as happened at the crucifixion of Christ, and will happen again during the Tribulation. These judgements would result in great mourning and lamentation, and the normal joyful festivals and singing would cease. Everyone would put on sackcloth and make their heads bald to indicate their sorrow and repentance. The scene would be like that of a family who are mourning for an only son who has died. The end of that day will be very bitter.

Then, in verses 11-14, the sovereign Lord GOD predicts that the days are going to come when He would cause there to be a desperate spiritual famine throughout the land of Israel for the word of God. This probably means that there will be no-one available to communicate the word of God. It is likely that the severe judgements mentioned in the previous few verses will have the effect of awakening many to a sense of spiritual need, but this hunger for the word of God will not be satisfied. Many will search the whole land from east to west, and from north to south for someone who can explain the truth of God to them, and they will fail to find anyone. Fair young women and strong young men, the younger generation, will faint because their thirst for truth and reality cannot be met. This implies that the older generation did not in their day communicate the truth to them, having sadly despised and rejected it themselves.

In verse 14, the LORD says that those who at that time were swearing by the sinful counterfeit worship of the altar at Samaria, Jeroboam's substitute religion, with its idols at Dan and Beersheba, would collapse and not recover from their fall. False religion is spiritually bankrupt and cannot help us in times of real need such as this will be. People are in desperate straits when God has nothing further to say to them, because they persistently rejected His word in previous years. Let us, therefore, in our day of plentiful opportunities to read, possess, and hear ministry on the Scriptures prize highly our great privileges in so doing, and not turn aside from them like ancient Israel to false gods, whatever form these may take.

Amos chapter 9

This final chapter of the prophecy includes two sharply contrasting sections. First, verses 1-10 complete the predictions concerning the destruction of the idolatrous system of religion at Bethel, and the almost total slaughter of the citizens of the Northern Kingdom of Israel as the LORD's punishment for their apostasy and wickedness. However, the final five verses of the chapter, and of the whole prophecy of Amos, promise the ultimate restoration of Israel in the future Millennial Kingdom, and the restoration of the Davidic dynasty also. Thus the book ends, as so often the prophetical books do, with a clear note of hope and salvation for the LORD's chosen earthly people Israel, after their tragic history of failure and disaster before this. As the apostle Paul said in Romans chapter 11 verse 29, 'the gifts and calling of God are without repentance'. God will fulfil His word to the patriarchs of Israel, and therefore we can expect Him to fulfil His promises to us as New Testament Christians today, in spite our own failures. Praise His Name!

1. The fifth, and concluding, vision of the sovereign Lord GOD destroying the idolatrous altar at Bethel, and announcing the inescapable judgements upon His sinful people Israel, yet saving a small remnant of them, vv. 1-10.

In verse 1, Amos saw the sovereign Lord, *Adonai*, standing in his vision beside, not actually upon, the altar at Bethel, where the Northern Kingdom worshipped the idolatrous calf images set up by Jeroboam the son of Nebat. The Lord commanded that the capitals be struck, so that the thresholds would be shaken and broken on the heads of all the worshippers there. Then He said that He would kill the rest of the idol worshippers with the sword, undoubtedly referring to that of the imminent invaders from Assyria, so that there would be no fugitives who could flee and preserve their lives.

In verses 2-4, the LORD asserted that, though the citizens of Israel should attempt to escape by digging into Sheol, or ascending into heaven, He would bring them up or down from there, and kill them. He is omnipresent, omniscient, and omnipotent. None of us can expect to escape from Him, as even the disobedient prophet Jonah found. Therefore, we should never attempt to do so, but rather should turn and face Him honestly with our problems, which only He can solve. Some Israelites might try to hide on the top of Mount Carmel with all its caves and forests, but He would search them out from there also. Nor would the floor of the sea be a safe hiding place, for He would command the serpent to bite them there, so that they died. Even if they went into captivity chased by their enemies, He would command that they be killed with the sword there. Wherever they went, He would see that they suffered harm, not good, from the invading Assyrians. There never is any hiding place for sinners from the sight of God, as Adam and Eve discovered in the Garden of Eden after they had sinned for the first time.

In verses 5-6, Amos considers the absolute power and majesty of the sovereign, eternal, covenant-keeping Lord GOD to inflict the terrible judgement described in the previous verses on His wayward people Israel in the Northern Kingdom. He is able to touch the earth and cause it to melt with volcanoes and earthquakes, so that many mourn the deaths these cause, while, at other times, He causes the waters to rise above their normal level in tsunamis, which are like the annual inundation of the River Nile in Egypt. He is in complete control of the heavens also. The RV translation of verse 6 should be preferred: 'it is He that buildeth His chambers in the heaven, and hath founded His vault upon the earth'. He controls the water cycle, which draws up the waters of the sea, and deposits them in rainclouds on the land. The name of the One who does all this is the LORD, yes, Israel's covenant-God, who is about to execute His wrath on His wicked people. They can never escape from Him; their fate is sealed.

Then, in verses 7-8, the LORD says that He is going to treat Israel just like the Gentile heathen nations around them, since they had been behaving no differently from them. For a time He is going to disown them. He will treat them like the Ethiopians. Not only did He bring up Israel from Egypt, but He also brought up the Philistines from Caphtor, or Crete, and the Syrians from Kir, whose location is now not identifiable. He controls all the movements of nations anyway, so why were Israel to be treated any differently from them, in view of their ungodly conduct? He had wanted them to be different from the other nations in many ways, but they had not complied with His desires for them, so why should they be spared as His special people any longer? God is no respecter of persons, and, when His own people disobey Him, He will punish them also.

The 'sinful kingdom' mentioned in verse 8 as the particular object of the LORD's wrath is here the Northern Kingdom of Israel. That whole evil regime would be destroyed and never restored; its kingdom would simply disappear from the map. However, and this is the first note of hope in the whole book, the LORD promises that He would not utterly destroy 'the house of Jacob', which name reminds us of Jacob's former dishonest character, before the LORD encountered him at Peniel, and began to change him forever. God has always preserved a small remnant of faithful believers in Israel, to whom He will ultimately fulfil His unconditional promises of grace and glory made to the patriarchs so long ago. Israel will never deserve their blessing, just as we today never will, but this all proves the complete faithfulness of God to His word to us, just as to His ancient people. Praise His Name!

Verses 9-10 summarise the LORD's dealings with Israel during all the many centuries since the days of Amos. He says through His servant that He will command that they be sifted among all nations, like grains of corn in a sieve. Yet not a single ear of grain will fall to the ground and be lost. However, the unrepentant and wicked sinners among them, who said that the calamity would never overtake or confront them, would all die by the sword. Ever since the exiles of Israel and Judah to Assyria and Babylon, respectively, this has been true of the LORD's earthly people, and it became even truer after the crucifixion of Christ, followed by the Jewish revolts of AD 70 and 125, including the destruction of Jerusalem with its temple by the Romans. The Jews have been wanderers among the nations, yet they have preserved their distinctive identity, and also survived numerous attempts to annihilate them, though millions of them have been slaughtered by the Gentile nations at times. The sifting process is continuing in our own days, and will not cease before they face the horrors of 'the time of Jacob's trouble' in the Tribulation years, but the LORD will see to it that a remnant of the nation is saved at last when Christ returns in glory to reign with them over the millennial earth.

2. The LORD through Amos promises that the Davidic Dynasty will be restored, and the nation of Israel regathered from captivity to their Promised Land and blessed during the Millennial Kingdom of Christ in eternal security from their former enemies, vv. 11-15.

Apart from parts of the previous three verses in this chapter, verses 11-15 are the only section of the prophecy of Amos which presents to Israel any real hope for their ultimate future. The first phrase of verse 11, 'in that day', tells them, and us, that this promise will only be fulfilled at the beginning of Christ's Millennial Kingdom, not before, and the previous few verses indicate that only a small remnant of the nation will enjoy the promised blessings outlined here. The apostates in the nation will all die before that time. The mention of 'the tabernacle of David' indicates that the Davidic dynasty, which reigned for several centuries in the Southern Kingdom of Judah, as opposed to the Northern Kingdom of Israel based in Samaria, is the one that the LORD is promising to raise up again, that is, to restore to the kingship lost in 586 BC to the Babylonian monarch Nebuchadnezzar. This will be fulfilled in the coming glorious reign of Christ Himself, who is the son of David, from Jerusalem for a thousand years in righteousness and peace. The restoration of the city of Jerusalem to its former glory looks well beyond the very partial return of the Jews after the Babylonian exile under Zerubbabel, Ezra, and Nehemiah right on to the end times. The LORD's gracious, and undeserved, promise is encouraging, because it proves that, although Israel has sunk to an all-time low today, so that judgement must fall on them, God's original purpose for the house of David, and His unconditional promises made to Abraham and his descendants have not failed, and will ultimately be fulfilled. Although Israel has been sadly marred, they are not beyond the LORD's ability to repair and restore. We need to consult other Scriptures to find that it will be the second coming of Christ in glory which will accomplish this miracle of grace; Amos does not mention this clearly here nor elsewhere in his book.

Verse 12 in the original Hebrew text indicates that the authority of Christ as Israel's final and true King will extend to all the Gentile nations, including the remnant of their most bitter enemy Edom, since He really owns all of them. That is the meaning of the phrase, 'which are called by my Name'; it denotes ownership. Christ will rightly rule over all the nations in the world in the Millennium.

Verses 11-12 are quoted by James, the Lord's half-brother, in Acts chapter 15 verses 16-18 at the co-called Council of Jerusalem, which was convened to consider the then vexed question of accepting Gentiles into the early Church, and on what terms, if any. There the quotation is not called by James a fulfilment of this prophecy in Amos, but an agreement with the words of the prophets generally, a general principle found throughout the prophets, and mentioned here in Amos also. In fact, James does not name Amos as the author of this quotation, nor does he quote from the words of the Hebrew Bible here, but from the Greek Septuagint translation of it, which differs in several important respects from the underlying Hebrew original text.

A literal translation of the original Hebrew text is as follows: 'In that day will I raise up the tabernacle of David that is fallen, and close up the breaches thereof; and I will raise up his ruins, and I will build it as in the days of old: that they may possess the remnant of Edom, and of all the heathen, which are called by My name, saith the LORD that doeth this'(AV/KJV). Compare this with the Greek Septuagint translation of Amos here, and you will see that the Greek translators were interpreting the Hebrew original in a completely different way. The latter, in Sir Lancelot Brenton's translation, reads as follows: 'In that day I will raise up the tabernacle of David that is fallen, and I will rebuild the ruins of it, and I will set up the parts thereof that have been broken down, and I will build it up as in the ancient days: that the remnant of men, and all the Gentiles upon whom My name is called, may earnestly seek Me, saith the Lord who does all these things'. Verse 12 is understood in a completely different way in the Greek translation from the clear meaning in the Hebrew original, which we have interpreted above. In particular, the word for 'Edom' in the Hebrew has been understood to be the very similar Hebrew word for 'man', that is *Adam*, as opposed to *Edom*, and the whole sense of the verse has been radically altered. In Acts chapter 15, verse 17, as alluded to by James, reads as follows: 'that the residue of men might seek after the LORD, and all the Gentiles, upon whom My name is called, saith the LORD, who doeth all these things' (AV/KJV). This is much nearer to the meaning of the Septuagint than the Hebrew original.

We conclude, therefore, that in Acts the verses are treated as an application of a general principle alluded to in the book of Amos, but not a primary interpretation of the words in that prophecy at all. This prophecy in Amos awaits a future fulfilment in the coming Millennial Kingdom of Christ, not in the Church today. James is simply saying that this passage in Amos highlights the general Biblical principle that the blessing of God is not exclusively reserved for the Jews, but Gentiles are also brought into blessing with them. This has always been the case, although the Jews have tended to reserve their privileges for themselves, and to exclude Gentiles altogether. The Jewish nation was always meant to act as a channel of blessing to all other nations, not as a stagnant and exclusive repository of Jewish privilege and blessing. In Isaiah chapter 43 verse 12, the LORD declared concerning Israel that, 'Ye are my witnesses, saith the LORD, that I am God', that is, to all the Gentile nations. In this task Israel has so far always failed very badly, and it will not be until God has saved His 144,000 Jewish witnesses at the beginning of the future Tribulation that they will really begin to fulfil it well, see Revelation chapter 7. However, this is not the real subject of these two verses in the original Hebrew text of Amos chapter 9.

At this point we reflect that the way in which the New

Testament inspired writers refer to the Old Testament is a very interesting and difficult study, since then the Holy Spirit was still writing Scripture, and was free to adapt previous Scriptures to support His teaching in the Age of Grace. We today are not justified in exercising that divine and sovereign freedom with the text of Scripture, but should always seek to interpret all Scripture alike in the most literal way that is reasonable. Here the literal sense of the Hebrew text is quite clear and reasonable, the one that we have given already, so that must be its primary interpretation. The Greek translators' quite different understanding of it is interesting, and has been made much of in Acts chapter 15, but is really irrelevant to our task of understanding the verses we are commenting on here in the Hebrew Bible.

To return, therefore, to the explanation of the book of Amos chapter 9 in the Hebrew text, verse 13 predicts the greatly increased fertility and productivity of the earth during the coming Millennial Kingdom of Christ. There will be many more grain and grape harvests every year, and even the mountains and hills, which are now usually not as fertile as the valleys, will flow with sweet wine, for the curse on creation will then have been removed, and the sun will shine seven times more brightly than it does now. It will be 'Paradise regained' in many respects. These promises should be understood quite literally, despite their slightly figurative expression. The Promised Land, and all the earth, will not only 'flow with milk and honey', but even the new wine that gives joy to mankind will cascade from the mountains in great abundance.

Then, finally, in verses 14-15, the LORD through Amos promises to restore the captivity of His people Israel from all parts of the world where they have been scattered for many centuries, and enable them to rebuild their desolated cities, and inhabit them in complete security from their former enemies. Their land, as indeed all parts of the world at that time, will have recently been ravaged by many invading armies and by God's direct supernatural judgements during the immediately preceding Tribulation, but when the world's rightful KING OF KINGS AND LORD OF LORDS, the Lord Jesus Christ, is established upon the throne of David in Jerusalem, there will be peace throughout the earth for a thousand years. Everything that sin has disturbed and destroyed will be restored, including the LORD's chosen earthly people Israel, represented by a small, but believing, remnant who will have waited for Him, and been born again in the day when He returns to deliver them from their enemies and to rule in perfect righteousness. Never again will they be uprooted from their Promised Land, which the LORD their God has given to them, however undeservedly, and they will long enjoy the fruit of their vineyards and the gardens which they will cultivate. This will be in contrast with the judgement of the extortioners in Israel mentioned in chapter 5 verse 11, who would not benefit from their houses and vineyards which they had built and planted by unrighteous methods. It will not be absolute perfection. That will only be achieved during the subsequent Day of God, eternity in the new heaven and the new earth, but the Millennial Kingdom of Christ will be the prelude to eternity. Only then will righteousness not just reign, but dwell eternally throughout the new universe.

Thus, the burden of Amos, the prophet who preached practical righteousness, ends with a clear note of hope and joy throughout Israel's Promised Land, because their true Davidic King, Christ Himself, will be reigning without a rival throughout the world from Jerusalem. Nearly all of his prophecy is marked by condemnation of mankind's unrighteousness, especially that of God's chosen earthly people Israel, but ultimately it is God's purpose to rectify this by regenerating the hearts of all who enter His Millennial Kingdom, so that they are able to live righteous lives before Him. We, who are Christian believers today during the Age of Grace and the New Testament Church, are already able to fulfil the righteous requirement of the Law in the power and enabling of the indwelling Holy Spirit, whom we received at the moment of conversion by faith in Christ.

Therefore, seeing that we look for such things, we should be diligent that we be found by our Lord and Saviour in peace and righteousness, as the apostle Peter instructed us in his second letter. We should be marked by constant acts of righteousness, not selfish acts of sin, and characterised by holiness and godliness in every part of our lives. Then we will be ready to wear our wedding garment at the coming Marriage of the Lamb, and rejoice the heart of our heavenly Bridegroom, the Lord Jesus, when we are united to Him in heaven. The searching message of the prophecy of Amos is that we should, by contrast with ancient Israel, be full of good works and practical acts of righteousness. How true is this of us individually today?

OBADIAH

Obadiah, the Prophet who Condemned Edom's Pride and Anti-Semitism

Introduction to Obadiah's Prophecy

Its Canonical Setting, Historical Background, and Possible Date

The Prophecy of Obadiah, which is the shortest book in the Old Testament, having only twenty-one verses, has always been placed as the fourth book in the Hebrew Book of the Twelve Minor Prophets, after Amos and before Jonah. We do not now know the logic behind the traditional Jewish ordering of these smaller books of the Old Testament, but some of them appear to have been placed in a roughly chronological order, beginning with the earlier prophets, and certainly ending with the later, post-exilic prophets, Haggai, Zechariah, and Malachi. This fact, by itself, would suggest that Obadiah was thought to have prophesied somewhat earlier than many of the other prophets whose books are listed after his book in the Hebrew canon. His book has been placed before Nahum, Habakkuk, and Zephaniah, who are all known to have prophesied not long before the Fall of Jerusalem to the Babylonians in 586 BC.

This fact is important to note, because some commentators have, quite understandably in view of some of the contents of his short prophecy, thought that Obadiah prophesied just after the beginning of the Babylonian Exile in 586 BC, while others have thought that he may have prophesied much earlier, at a time when Jerusalem had been attacked and plundered by the Philistines and Arabians during the reign of Jehoram, a wicked king of Judah (ca. 852-841 BC), in the middle of the ninth century BC. Then the Edomites had revolted against Judah, and the LORD caused these allies of theirs to attack

His wayward people, see 2 Chronicles 21. 8-20. Also, it does seem likely that Obadiah wrote his book before the ministry of Jeremiah just prior to the Babylonian Exile, since Jeremiah chapter 49 verses 7-22 is very similar to much of Obadiah, although not the same word for word, and probably dependent upon it, not vice versa. Furthermore, in Obadiah's book there are no examples of Aramaic expressions, which would tend to support a later date. Finally, the Gentile nations mentioned in Obadiah, namely, the Philistines and the Canaanites, are pre-exilic, not post-exilic, enemies of Israel, nor is there any mention of the Assyrians or Babylonians, who were their captors in the two exiles.

However, we cannot be certain that Obadiah did not write about the time of the Babylonian Exile, nor that the order of the Twelve Minor Prophets is so strictly chronological as may be thought likely. The message of his prophecy is more important to consider and apply to ourselves today than the exact historical background and date of the book. As we shall see, the searching message of Obadiah is quite clear and plain for all to understand.

Its Authorship

The prophecy is entitled, in the first verse, 'the vision of Obadiah'. His name means 'the servant or worshipper of the LORD', and occurs about a dozen times in the Old Testament, but none of the other men called Obadiah appear to be the same as the author of this book. We know nothing more concerning this prophet called Obadiah than what we can deduce from the meaning of his name and the contents of his short prophecy. His message as the servant of the LORD is, again, more important than any details about his life and ministry. There seems to be no good reason why we should doubt that he was the sole author, under the inspiration of the Holy Spirit of God, of this book, just as there is no good reason to doubt that Malachi, whose name simply means 'My messenger', was the genuine author of that later prophecy. Most of the other writing prophets are described by a short genealogy or epithet, but not all. The LORD's message through them is paramount, and we should listen to His voice to us today, just as Israel were expected to listen to His humble servants in their days.

Its Outline

We present here three outlines of Obadiah selected from the commentaries consulted in writing. They are as follows:

First, the summary outline in the *MacArthur Bible Commentary*:

Outline
i. God's Judgment on Edom (1-14)
   A. Edom's Punishment (1-9)
   B. Edom's Crimes (10-14)
ii. God's Judgment on the Nations (15,16)
iii. God's Restoration of Israel (17-21)

Secondly, the helpful outline in Sidlow Baxter's *Explore the Book*:

THE BOOK OF OBADIAH
THE PROPHET OF POETIC JUSTICE
1. <u>THE DESTRUCTION OF EDOM (verses 1-16).</u>
   THE CERTAINTY OF IT, verses 1-9.
   THE REASON FOR IT, verses 10-16.

2. <u>THE SALVATION OF ISRAEL (verses 17-21).</u>
   THE PROMISE OF IT, verses 17-18.
   THE FULNESS OF IT, verses 19-21.

Thirdly, the fuller analysis in the *Bible Knowledge Commentary*:

OUTLINE
i. Edom's Destruction (vv. 1-9)
   A. The call to the nations to destroy Edom (v. 1)
   B. The prophecy of Edom's destruction (vv. 2-9)
      1. Edom's pride to be debased (vv. 2-4)
      2. Edom's wealth to be plundered (vv. 5-7)
      3. Edom's people to be slaughtered (vv. 8-9)
ii. Edom's Crimes (vv. 10-14)
   A. Violation in attitudes (vv. 10-12)
   B. Violations in actions (vv. 13-14)
iii. God's Judgment on Israel's Enemies (vv. 15-16)
iv. God's Blessings on Israel's People (vv. 17-21)

A. The deliverance of Israel (vv. 17-18)
B. The delineation of Israel's territories (vv. 19-20)
C. The establishment of the Lord's kingdom (v. 21)

Its Main Searching Message

The main searching message for us today from the prophecy of Obadiah is two-fold: first, the sinfulness and folly of pride, such as caused Edom to think that they were superior to others, and practically invincible in their mountain fortresses, such as Sela, later named Petra, in Mount Seir. Secondly, the wickedness and downfall of anti-Semitism, racial hatred against Israel, such as Edom had always displayed towards his brother-nation Israel, the descendants of his twin Jacob from the moment of their conception in Rebekah's womb. Obadiah here condemns both sinful attitudes, and predicts, first, the judgement and downfall of Edom and, secondly, the restoration of Israel to their kingdom in the Millennial Age.

Pride is both wrong and foolish. Lucifer originally fell through pride, and trying to usurp the place that belonged to God alone. He has passed this original sin on to all mankind, many of whom down the centuries have attempted to displace God from His throne, and rule the world to fulfil their own selfish ambitions in either smaller or much wider spheres of influence. In the coming Tribulation, the Man of Sin, the Beast of Revelation chapter 13, will try to claim that he is God, to rule the whole world as his own domain, and to persecute all who trust in God. That is where mankind's sin of pride is leading him. Beware of this deadly sin, and seek to cultivate a truly humble attitude to all others, including God, in all departments of our lives. Consider that God is the only ultimate source of all that we are, have, and are able to do, and not ourselves or our own ability at all. We are simply responsible to Him to hold our God-given gifts in stewardship for His glory, and to use and develop these in His strength alone. We should never parade ourselves, nor imagine that we are better, or more important, than anyone else, but in due humility worship Him, the God of all grace, alone! He is fully able to humble us, just as He did, and will, humble the Edomites with the greatest of ease. We are all so weak and puny before His divine majesty and sovereignty. Let us learn this lesson the easier way, by precept, rather than by bitter experience. Pride always goes before a fall!

Many of the nations in our own day have failed to learn the second lesson taught to us by Obadiah's short prophecy, namely, that opposition to Israel is futile and counter-productive. Israel, despite their many sins and apostasy from their covenant-keeping LORD God, is the apple of God's eye, the earthly nation which He has especially chosen to use in fulfilling His purposes of salvation and judgement in the world through Christ. In the Middle East, and throughout most parts of the world, anti-Semitism is rife even now, and will be until Christ comes again in glory to reign. Jerusalem is a 'burdensome stone to all nations', as Zechariah prophesied that it would be in chapter 12 of his prophecy, the chief international problem faced by world governments and statesmen of all nations. Israel, and Christians today, are just waiting for Christ to come back and restore the situation in His own time, as Scripture predicts that He will.

The Edomites needed to learn this lesson in their day, having bitterly opposed and hated their brother-nation from the earliest times right up to Obadiah's day. They have nursed their hatred ever since Esau chose to surrender his birthright to Jacob for 'a mess of pottage'. Esau himself seems to have forgiven Jacob for his deception and trickery, since he did not value spiritual things in any way, but his Edomite descendants have never forgiven Jacob's descendants for this sin. When Moses requested that the Israelites might pass quietly and quickly through Edomite territory on the way to their Promised Land, the Edomites curtly refused to comply with this, and made their relatives do a large detour around their country. God had told Israel not to hate their brother, since he was related to them, but the Edomites had not reciprocated their kindness. For centuries since then there had been constant friction, and frequent wars, between Edom and Israel, as the historical books bear out. However, this small book of Obadiah assures us of the eventual outcome of this opposition to Israel, namely, that God will decisively judge Edom for it. Since God is against them, they have never had any hope of ultimate victory in this conflict, nor have Gentile nations today. History records that those Gentile nations who have supported Israel, have been providentially blessed by God, and protected from much evil that has befallen other opposing nations. As the apostle Paul said concerning Christians today in Romans chapter 8 verse 31, 'If God be for us, who can be against us?' Let us today love the Jews, as God does, and pray for the peace of Jerusalem.

Sidlow Baxter points out that Obadiah is the prophet of poetic justice. In verse 15, he says to Edom, 'As thou hast done, it shall be done unto thee'. This is the key to the meaning of the book, for Scripture warns us that we reap exactly what we sow, whether that is good or bad, see Galatians chapter 6. Edom had sown hatred and violence, and therefore was to receive judgement and destruction. Have we thoroughly learned this lesson, and sought to sow good to all around us?

Its Other Valuable Lessons

First, Obadiah presents Edom as a typical Gentile nation in its hostility towards God and His people. What is said here concerning Edom applies equally to all other nations who oppose Israel. There are a number of prophecies against Edom in the Old Testament, and in some of them Edom's final judgement seems to foreshadow Christ's conquest of all His enemies at the time when He comes in glory to reign in His Millennial Kingdom.

Secondly, Esau, and Edom, are illustrations of the flesh, our old natures, our 'natural man', in their pride and hostility towards God, who alone can subdue their evil desires and ambitions. Sidlow Baxter, again, points out that Esau is a type, or illustration, of our flesh, the nature we inherited from Adam, in its fairest form, attractive and lovable, but fiercely opposed to God. Esau was marked by physical grace and power; he was 'ruddy'. Yet he was also associated with Edom, 'the red one', which often in Scripture speaks of violence. Edom is actually a form of the word Adam. In Hebrews chapter 12, the writer says that Esau despised his birthright, thought it of no value by comparison with his craving for red stew at the time to satisfy his hunger. The man after the flesh has no time for spiritual things and sees no point in pursuing them; he wants only carnal things that he can immediately see and use to gratify his own selfish natural appetites. Therefore, Christians today need to make no provision for the flesh to fulfil its evil desires, but to mortify the deeds of the body in self-judgement. Instead, we should set our affections on things above, in heaven, where Christ sits at the right hand of God. These are further valuable lessons which are illustrated by the prophecy of Obadiah. How far have we learned them?

Thus the prophecy of Obadiah teaches us many valuable spiritual lessons which we need to learn thoroughly today in our own materialistic, pleasure-seeking age, which is very hostile to God and His claims upon us, and also hostile to His people, whether in earthly Israel or the New Testament Church of true believers. God will ultimately have the last word, and humble all our pride and judge all opposition to Israel and the Church. Edom, and all that they represent will be finally judged, while the true saints will triumph when Christ returns to set up His everlasting kingdom on earth.

Furthermore, since Edom is linguistically related to the name Adam, the head of our whole fallen and sinful race, we see in this little book of Obadiah a salutary warning concerning the evil potential of our old natures, and also their ultimate fate. Obadiah graphically illustrates our own sinful natures, and the sight is most unpleasant. In Romans chapter 8 we read that God will judge them finally at the Resurrection and Rapture of the Church, when the redemption of our bodies will be accomplished, and our final salvation completed by having our sinful natures eradicated from our beings. Therefore, let us not now yield to their temptations, since they are doomed, and seek the help of God's Holy Spirit within us to do so. He it is who alone can enable us to live lives of victory over sin now, something that Edom and ancient Israel, sadly, did not have. Praise the LORD for His present grace to us today!

Concise Commentary on Obadiah

1. The LORD's announcement through Obadiah that Edom will be judged for their pride, vv. 1-9.

Verse 1 begins with the title of the book, namely, 'the vision of Obadiah'. Obadiah not only heard the LORD speaking to him, but evidently saw a vision of Him doing so. This little book is a real revelation, a message of God from His immediate presence, as all messages should be. His message is from the sovereign Lord GOD, *Adonai Jehovah*, Israel's eternal, faithful, covenant-keeping God, who brought them out of Egypt to be His own special nation for eternity. The message concerns Edom, their implacable enemy, but actually related to them through their forefather Jacob, Esau's younger twin brother.

What then is the LORD's message? It is that, 'we', which may well include all Obadiah's fellow-prophets, 'have heard a rumour from the LORD, and an ambassador is sent among the heathen, Arise ye, and let us rise up against her in battle'. The message is therefore a declaration of the LORD's intention to judge Edom through the united action of several Gentile nations. God often initiates such judgement by means of unsaved people, and even by means of lying spirits, who deceive the latter into taking this action. That occurred in the case of Ahab's death in battle in 1 Kings chapter 22, and it will happen again when God wishes to draw all the nations into battle at Armageddon to their destruction, according to Revelation chapter 16. He is in complete control of the whole universe, good and evil included, although He is not responsible for the evil that His creatures commit against Him, but will judge it. In His overruling sovereignty, He makes even the wrath of man to praise Him. How great God is!

Part of verse 1 is clearly quoted in Jeremiah chapter 49 verse 14 concerning the LORD's intention to destroy Edom; only, Jeremiah substitutes the pronoun 'I' at the beginning, referring to himself, rather than 'we' here, probably meaning Obadiah and all his fellow-prophets. See the Introduction for a discussion of the probable relative dates of Obadiah and Jeremiah.

In verse 2, the LORD speaks directly to Edom concerning their imminent judgement, 'Behold, I have made thee small among the heathen (nations): thou art greatly despised', which predicts the result of the LORD's coming judgemental action against them. The verb 'I have made thee', is a 'prophetic perfect' in the original Hebrew, which means that the future action predicted is as good as accomplished already in the mind of God, so certain is it to be fulfilled. It could therefore be translated correctly as, 'I will make thee small among the nations', as some more recent translators have decided to do. History, both Biblical and secular, bears witness to the partial fulfilment of this judgement already, but Scripture further predicts the final judgement of Edom when Christ returns in glory to reign, according to Isaiah chapters 34 and 63. They will be one of the last nations to be subjugated by the Lord Jesus then, as one of His chief enemies. Their land will be one of the few areas of the world to be left desolate during the Millennial Kingdom as evidence of the LORD's judgement, and as a perpetual warning to all nations then of the folly of rebellion against God. Have we learned this lesson thoroughly yet?

In verses 3 and 4, we learn the salutary lesson that the innate pride of our natural hearts deceives us into thinking that we are invincible, just as Edom vainly thought that their mountain fortresses were impregnable against all attack by their enemies. Lucifer, the original father of lies, imagined that he could usurp the throne of his God, because there was no-one as beautiful as he was in the rest of creation. His spiritual children in Edom thought the same. How wrong he was, as Isaiah chapter 14 and Ezekiel chapter 28 bear witness! Edom have ever since had to learn their real weakness, and will yet need to recognise the full truth about themselves before God. The defences of Edom were repeatedly overrun by a succession of enemies used by the LORD to judge them: first, the Assyrians; then the Babylonians; later, the Nabateans from Arabia, the Maccabees, and the Romans. They had tried to exalt themselves to the heavens in the imagined security of Sela, their rock city with a very narrow entrance in a ravine, but the LORD was soon to bring them down to earth by providential means, using other nations to do so.

Thankfully, Christian believers have begun to learn this necessary lesson in our own day, usually in an easier way than Edom both did and will. Sadly, many unbelievers never learn it in this life. Pride, arrogance, and conceit are all natural to our old natures, and consequently are thought not to be reprehensible by the world around us. Humility, lowliness of mind, and self-judgement are all thought by most men to be weaknesses of character, not strengths at all, but the Scriptures teach otherwise throughout their pages. They cite the supreme example of the Lord Jesus Christ, the Son of God incarnate, in several places in the epistles, not to mention the Gospel records of His life and ministry. As Christian disciples, believers today should follow Him in every way!

Then, verses 5-9 predict how thoroughly Edom will come unstuck in their false security of possessions, allies, human wisdom, and military strength. First, in verses 5-6, Obadiah predicts that Edom will lose all its accumulated wealth. The invading armies will not just be satisfied to take the most valuable, or most accessible, possessions, like robbers breaking into a house at night, who, after they think that they have taken enough for themselves, leave the rest of the house untouched. No, they will remove everything. Nor will they be like grape-gatherers, who usually leave some gleanings behind for others to harvest. No, absolutely everything in Edom will go, including all their hidden treasures. Edom was on some important caravan trade routes, and had become quite rich by profiting from this international trade, but all their wealth would be taken away, so that they would be destitute.

Secondly, verse 7 reveals that even Edom's allies, who had made peace with them in the past, who had even been supported by them at one time, will deceive them, turn against them, and drive them out of their country into captivity. Their treachery will bring about Edom's downfall. Edom, which was once renowned for its human wisdom, gained through contact with other countries along the trade routes, would be seen not to have exercised sufficient discernment in their choice of allies after all. Their city of Teman was noted for its wise men, such as Eliphaz the Temanite in the book of Job, but their real foolishness would be manifest to all the world, when their wise men were destroyed, and they were completely humiliated. Trust in God alone, not in any man, however great or wise!

Verse 8 uses the phrase 'in that day', which probably refers to 'the day of the LORD'. In Scripture, this can refer either to the ultimate future day of the LORD, or to an Old Testament day of the LORD, when He has previously intervened in a nation's affairs to assert His authority and judge them. Here in Obadiah it could mean either intervention, both a now past intervention, and the future final intervention by Christ at His appearing in glory to judge and reign, for both will prove to be true. As mentioned above, Edom has already been judged several times by foreign invaders, but there is coming a final invasion just before the setting up of Christ's Millennial Kingdom.

Thirdly, verse 9 predicts that all Edom's mighty men from Teman, their military might in which they trusted, would be dismayed when the invaders came, and slaughtered. Edom would find that they had no adequate national defence. The once proud nation would be humbled at last by the LORD's sovereign overruling intervention. Let Christian believers today rather humble themselves under the mighty hand of God, that He may exalt us in His own time and way, for His glory, not ours!

2. The LORD through Obadiah explains the crimes of violence which Edom had committed against Israel, their brother-nation, and for which they would soon be judged, vv. 10-14.

Now the LORD explains why Edom will be judged so severely; it is because they have so often acted with violence against their brother-nation, the descendants of Jacob. Edom never forgave them for their forefather's deceptions in taking from Esau both his birthright and his blessing, and nursed continual hatred against them, which sometimes broke out in active aggression. This is why they would be covered with shame and eventually be destroyed for ever as a nation. Envy turns to hatred, and results in murder so often in daily life. Christian believers today still need to guard against such serious sins, both individually and within assembly life. An unforgiving spirit against our brethren and sisters in the Lord can so easily disrupt and completely destroy all true fellowship, and leads to the removal of the assembly by God altogether because our testimony is so bad. Fellow-saints, beware, repent, and seek reconciliation if at all possible!

The LORD now rehearses some specific sins of violence that Edom had committed against Israel. First, in verse 11, He condemns them for standing aloof, and on the other side of the battle, when foreign invaders carried away Israel's military forces captive, and when the latter subsequently entered Jerusalem and cast lots among themselves for particular parts of the city they had captured. Edom had failed to help their closely-related nation, which was a sin of omission. We do not now know which particular incident in Israel's history this refers to, whether the earlier occasion mentioned in the Introduction during the reign of Jehoram in the ninth century BC, or perhaps the later occasion, when Jerusalem was besieged and destroyed by the Babylonians under Nebuchadnezzar in 586 BC, but it could apply to either occasion.

Then, in verses 12-14, the LORD lists about eight ways in which the Edomites had committed a serious sin on such an occasion, telling them that they should not have done certain specific reprehensible things against their brother-nation. They should not have gloated over their brethren's misfortune when they were attacked, nor found any pleasure in seeing their destruction. They should not have boasted when their city fell to their enemies, and they should certainly not have joined with the invaders in entering Jerusalem on the day it was captured, in order to loot their wealth. No, nor should they have stood in the fork in the road outside the captured city, in order to deliberately cut off their brethren's escape from the city to safety, and then to imprison their survivors in the day of their distress.

No, it is never right to rejoice over, or take advantage of, our enemies' downfall; rather, we should do everything to help them, if we can. This applies equally to believers today. We should not rejoice over misfortunes that befall either our persecutors or our fellow-brethren who have wronged us in some way. That is not the spirit of Christ; He prayed for those who were crucifying Him, that His Father might forgive them. We should pray for the salvation of all our most sworn enemies in a spirit of self-sacrificial love. We should never try to 'get our own back', which, sadly, is an expression all too commonly heard. Instead, we should seek our persecutors' positive good and blessing, and leave all necessary vengeance to God in His own time and way.

3. Obadiah declares the nearness of the Day of the LORD's invention in judgement to recompense all nations, including Edom, justly for their sins, with the result that Edom would be destroyed by other Gentile nations in a way similar to that in which they had destroyed Israel, vv. 15-16.

Having just enumerated Edom's many sins, for which they would be punished, the LORD through Obadiah turns to consider the implications of His future intervention to judge all nations, including Edom, Israel's most persistent enemy, in the future Day of the LORD. He declares the inevitable principle which He will apply to them all, namely, that, 'as thou hast done, it shall be done unto thee', which is an eternal moral law of life in God's world. The Lord Jesus told His disciples the closely related principle, that they should always do as they would be done by, the so-called 'golden rule' for life. Throughout Scripture we are warned that we will reap exactly what we sow in our lives, whether that is good or evil, see Galatians chapter 6. All nations will also learn this the hard way, when Christ returns in glory to judge and reign over this world, and Obadiah says that that day is near. This will definitely apply to Edom, who will find that their evil conduct will rebound, like a boomerang, upon their own heads to destroy them.

In part this has already happened to them, as we have previously mentioned, in the successive invasions that they experienced during the Old Testament and Inter-Testamental periods, but their final demise awaits the future coming of Christ, as Isaiah chapters 34 and 63 predict. At that time, during the final part of the Tribulation, Edom will have joined the final great alliance formed to oppose Israel and the returning Christ, but they will be completely defeated soon after Christ returns. Just as they had 'drunk upon' the LORD's 'holy mountain' in Jerusalem, in the sense that they had celebrated Israel's downfall, exactly so would all the surrounding Gentile nations 'drink continually' from them, celebrating Edom's demise with glee, and, by the beginning of the Millennial Kingdom, Edom would be so completely obliterated from the world's map that it would appear that they had never existed.

4. The LORD predicts the final future salvation and restoration of Israel to a position of supremacy over Edom, and the establishment of His Millennial Kingdom over Edom, just as over the rest of the world, vv. 17-21.

As in so many of the prophetical books of Scripture, Obadiah's prophecy ends on a very high and hopeful note for Israel, His chosen earthly people, by contrast with its predicted downfall and destruction of their longest-standing and worst enemy, Edom.

Verse 17 begins with the assurance that, by contrast with Edom, who will be completely destroyed, 'upon Mount Zion shall be deliverance', or 'those who escape', that is, 'a remnant', as always in God's sovereign gracious purposes for Israel, however undeservedly. The next phrase, 'and there shall be holiness', is better translated 'and it will be holy', referring to Mount Zion. 'And the house of Jacob shall possess their possessions', that is, the whole of the land promised to them in the time of Abraham, by contrast with the small portion of it that they have ruled over for most of their previous history. The name 'Jacob' is used here, because it reminds us that he was Esau's favoured younger brother, and because his inheritance has always been quite undeserved in view of his crooked nature and deceitful dealings with Esau and others. Also, 'Mount Zion' reminds us of the LORD's unconditional covenant with David, to whom He promised an everlasting dynasty and kingdom in 2 Samuel chapter 7.

Then, in verse 18, the LORD predicts that the houses, or peoples, of Jacob and Joseph will act as a consuming fire of judgement against the house, or dynasty, of Esau, who will be completely destroyed by them as easily as stubble, so that there will not be any survivors left in Edom at all. This is the LORD's considered sentence of judgement against them which cannot be revoked or avoided. Several other Scriptures explain that Israel will be the LORD's means of destroying Edom in the end times, when the Lord Jesus returns to take up His great power and reign; see Isaiah chapters 11, 34, and 63, Ezekiel chapter 25, and Daniel chapter 11, in particular.

Verses 19-20 explain the full extent of Israel's possessions in their Promised Land in more detail, particularly as they relate to their enemies' former territories. The Israelites who live in the southern region known as the Negev will possess the Mount of Esau, while those who live in the western maritime lowlands known as the Shephelah will possess the former territory of the Philistines. Those who live further north will possess the territory of Ephraim, including Samaria, which was once the capital of the Northern Kingdom of Israel in the days of the Divided Kingdom, while the tribe of Benjamin will possess the north-eastern region of Gilead, which is part of Transjordan.

Verse 20 has been understood in more than one way by commentators. This is because it is uncertain as to how it should be translated. A few words may need to be added in translation to clarify the sense. We quote two fairly reliable versions, bracketing the words which have been added in translation. First, the RV, thus: 'And the captivity of this host of the children of Israel, which are [among] the Canaanites, [shall possess] even unto Zarephath; and the captivity of Jerusalem, which is in Sepharad, shall possess the cities of the South.' Secondly, the NASB, as follows: 'And the exiles of this host of the sons of Israel, who are [among] the Canaanites as far as Zarephath, and the exiles of Jerusalem who are in Sepharad, will possess the cities of the Negev'. Certainly, the 'captivity' means the surviving exiles of Israel in the end times. They will possess the Promised Land as far north as Zarephath, modern Sarafand in Lebanon between Tyre and Sidon, and as far south as the Negev. The location of Sepharad is unknown, but today, and throughout the Middle Ages, the 'Sephardi' Jews have been understood to come from the Mediterranean area, Southern Europe, and North Africa. At all events, the returning Jewish remnant at the beginning of the Millennial Kingdom will possess their Promised Land in its entirety.

In verse 21, Obadiah's prophecy rises to a great final triumphant crescendo, when he predicts, under the inspiration of the Holy Spirit, that at that time, the end time, when Christ returns to reign, 'saviours', or better, deliverers like the Old Testament judges, will come up on Mount Zion to judge the Mount of Esau, once and for all subduing their opposition to His people Israel, 'and the kingdom shall be the LORD's'. Edom will never again exist as an independent, self-governing nation, but be completely subjugated to the LORD's Christ through delegated rulers on Mount Zion in Jerusalem, which will become the world's capital city, restored and elevated above its present altitude. Then will be fulfilled the vision given to the apostle John in Revelation chapter 11 verse 15, 'the kingdom of the world is become the kingdom of our Lord, and of His Christ: and He shall reign forever and ever' (RV).

> *'Jesus shall reign where'er the sun*
> *Doth his successive journeys run;*
> *His kingdom stretch from shore to shore*
> *Till moons shall wax and wane no more'.*
> Isaac Watts (1674-1748)
> Hallelujah! Praise the LORD!

Finally, let us seriously consider and apply the searching message of Obadiah's short prophecy to ourselves today. In the nation of Edom in Obadiah's prophecy we have seen an ugly picture of our evil old nature, their pride in our own supposed ability and invincibility, their envy of all that is good, their hatred of God's people and all His interests, and their desire to murder all whom they hate, as Edom did Israel, the LORD's chosen earthly people, however crooked, wayward, failing, and undeserving. Those desires still lie latent within us, even as true Christian believers today, shocking though the revelation may be to us. Paul learned the hard way that, 'in me (that is, in my flesh) dwelleth no good thing: for to will is present with me; but how to perform that which is good I find not', Romans 7. 18. Thankfully, Paul soon pointed all New Testament believers to the answer in Christ and the liberating power of the Holy Spirit, who now indwells every true Christian in the Age of Grace, but did not do so in Old Testament saints. 'For the law of the Spirit of life in Christ Jesus hath made me free from the law of sin and death', because God in the Person of His incarnate Son condemned sin in the flesh, the old Adam and Edom nature, at the cross, 'that the righteousness [righteous requirement] of the law might be fulfilled in us, who walk not after the flesh, but after the Spirit', see Romans 8. 1-4.

So for us today there is freedom from the enslaving power of our old evil Edom-nature through Christ as we respond in obedient faith to the constant promptings of God's Spirit within us towards humility, love, and all that is good, wholesome, and lovely. The old nature is condemned to death, and will be destroyed at the redemption of our bodies, when the Lord Jesus comes again and accomplishes our final salvation, but the new nature is eternal and perfect. Let us be warned, therefore, by the stark picture of our old nature presented in this part of Scripture, and avail ourselves of God's gracious provision for living a righteous and victorious Christian life today, until Christ comes to call us to Himself, and frees us forever from our present bodies of sin and death! Praise His Name!

JONAH

Jonah, the Most Successful, yet Most Disobedient, Prophet

Introduction to the Book of Jonah

Its Canonical Setting

The Book of Jonah has always been placed fifth in the canonical order of the Hebrew prophetical books which are known as 'The Twelve' Minor Prophets, all of whose messages have major significance, despite their small size. Jonah is tucked between the undated prophecy of Obadiah concerning the downfall of Edom, the shortest book in the Old Testament, and the later prophecy of Micah, who was a younger contemporary of the prophet Isaiah in the eighth century BC. Both Jonah and Micah prophesied in the days of the Assyrian Empire during the eighth century BC, as did the definitely later prophet Nahum, but the LORD led them to give rather different messages both to Israel and the Assyrians in their respective times of ministry. 'Jonah' means 'dove', the emblem of peace, while the number five, the position of his book within the Twelve Minor Prophets, in some Scriptures suggests the thought of grace, or perhaps human responsibility. Certainly, in the book of Jonah the LORD showed great mercy and grace towards the Assyrian people of Nineveh, who were Israel's worst enemies, and the prophet himself failed rather badly in his responsibility towards both the LORD and his hearers, and yet the LORD treated him with great mercy and grace. Thus the message of the book may be seen to be entirely appropriate to its canonical setting and the meaning of Jonah's name. At all events, it is a unique record of spiritual biography within the canon of Holy Scripture, and also within the prophetical books.

Introduction to the Book of Jonah

Its Historical Background and Date

The book of Jonah was clearly written in the days of the Assyrian Empire. The only other Old Testament reference to Jonah is 2 Kings chapter 14 verse 25, which states that Jonah the son of Amittai gave a predictive prophecy to Israel during the reign of Jeroboam II concerning the latter's recovery of much of the original territory possessed by the nation in the days of the United Monarchy under David and Solomon, between Hamath in the north near Lebanon and Syria and the sea of the Arabah, that is, the Dead Sea, in the south. Jeroboam II was actually an evil king, but the LORD allowed him to reign for forty-one years, between 793 and 752 BC, in the northern half of the Divided Kingdom. He had considerable military success in expanding his kingdom even beyond Damascus at a time when the power of Assyria was relatively weak and vulnerable to attack by various enemies.

However, despite the material affluence of the Northern Kingdom of Israel during his reign, its government and people became increasingly corrupt, idolatrous, and morally wicked. Therefore, the LORD had declared through prophets whose ministry may have overlapped with that of Jonah, notably Amos and Hosea, that He would use the Assyrians to judge His people Israel and carry them away into exile in Assyria. Certainly, Assyria was the greatest threat to Israel during that period of Israelite history, and Jonah knew this very well. He disliked the Assyrians intensely, because they were noted for being mercilessly cruel and barbarous in their conduct of wars of expansion. Therefore, he did not want them to be spared God's severe judgement, for his people Israel lay directly in the path of their ambitions.

His prophetic book can, therefore, be dated during the first half of the eighth century BC, some time before Assyria recovered from its period of weakness, and, under some vigorous kings, such as Tiglath-pileser III (745-727 BC), began to expand their empire into countries south of them, including Israel. A date around 760 BC is suggested by some commentators, and may be confirmed by other considerations explained below. The book itself gives no indication as to when and where it was written, but it is a very honest record of Jonah's earlier oral ministry to Assyria in the very heart of their empire, in Nineveh itself. Finally, M.F. Unger notes that the presence of some Aramaic linguistic expressions in the book is no clear guide to its date, since such expressions occur in the Hebrew Bible, and in Ugaritic literature, from about 1400 BC onwards. This is, therefore, no proof of a late date, which some commentators have suggested.

Its Authorship

The book of Jonah is written entirely in the third person, and appears to be anonymous. In this it is unique among the prophetical books, which elsewhere always include a note of authorship, however brief. In the book the prophet Jonah appears in a very unfavourable light with regard to his relationship with the LORD who sent him to Nineveh, and it ends with the LORD gently rebuking his unwilling and downcast servant for his unfortunate attitude towards the people of Assyria. Although his ministry to them was really a complete success, his conduct towards the LORD had been very disobedient; a striking paradox!

All this strongly suggests what has been the conclusion of most readers, namely, that Jonah himself wrote the book after he had returned from his mission to Assyria, and had responded favourably to the LORD's rebuke at the end of chapter 4. Some of the LORD's most faithful servants still find themselves on a steep learning curve during the fulfilment of their allotted ministries; they do not yet know it all, nor are they at all perfect! Jonah is here probably giving a very honest account of a bad patch in his ministry, when his relationship with the LORD was not as it should have been, but he did learn his lessons – the hard way! This is surely encouraging to us today, because we all do have times when we are not as obedient to the LORD as we should be. He is very patient with us, as He was with Jonah, and is still prepared to use us in His service, once we repent. Although we are left at the end of the book not knowing whether Jonah repented of his attitude, or not, the very existence of this book in Scripture strongly suggests that he did so.

Therefore, assuming that Jonah was the author of the book which bears his name, what do we know about him from 2 Kings chapter

Introduction to the Book of Jonah

14? First, that he was the son of Amittai, which means 'truthful', and that he came from a village called Gath-hepher, a few miles north-east of Nazareth in the territory of Zebulun, according to Joshua chapter 19 verse 13. This not very far from the Sea of Galilee. The enemies of the Lord Jesus were completely wrong when they asserted to Nicodemus, in John chapter 7 verse 52, that no prophet came from Galilee. Jonah had come from Galilee! Today in Israel, visitors are shown the traditional tomb of Jonah in the small village of el-Meshhed on the Tiberias road just a few miles out of Nazareth. This leads us on to consider the historicity of the book of Jonah, which has been much disputed by unbelievers.

Its Historicity

The historicity of the book of Jonah is confirmed by none other than the Lord Jesus Christ Himself in the Gospel records, for He spoke about Jonah as a real historical person, who not only spent three days and three nights in the belly of the great fish, but who was also instrumental in the repentance of the whole city of Nineveh; see Matthew 12. 39-41 and Luke 11. 29-32. If we doubt the objective truth of His words, then we doubt the historical basis of all Scripture, and prove that we are really unbelievers. There are miracles recorded throughout Scripture, and true believers gladly accept them as historically genuine, because they have proved the truth of the gospel in their own lives. We do not need to be able to explain, or understand, them, but we wholeheartedly believe what God has said in His Word of truth. The book of Jonah contains many miracles, which we can list here: the sudden storm at sea; the selection of Jonah as the guilty party by lot; the sudden subsiding of the storm to a great calm; the great fish appearing at exactly the right time to swallow Jonah; the preservation of Jonah in the belly of the fish; his ejection from its belly, safe and well, on the shore; the gourd; the worm; the sultry east wind; and the repentance of the entire city of Nineveh at the preaching of Jonah. If we remove the miraculous element from Scripture as a whole, we would have very little left. Absolute truth is often stranger to us than fiction. Once we accept the omnipotence of God, then everything else can be understood and accepted as entirely possible, because with God nothing is impossible; Luke 1. 37.

It is not surprising that Assyrian historians do not record the remarkable event of Nineveh's repentance at the preaching of Jonah, since the kings of Assyria would certainly regard this as a sign of great weakness. However, we have already referred to the fact that, at this time in their empire's history, the Assyrians were somewhat weaker in military strength than they were later in the eighth century BC, and that this had allowed Jeroboam II to expand his kingdom's boundaries to encroach on territory that the Assyrians later regained from other kingdoms. In a similar way, the later Assyrian king Sennacherib did not record his miraculous and catastrophic defeat in the siege of Jerusalem in 701 BC, but only stated that he had shut up Hezekiah inside Jerusalem 'like a bird in a cage'. These proud Gentile monarchs did not usually broadcast their failures. The inspired Hebrew historians were far more honest about such matters! At all events, the Assyrians knew that they were rather vulnerable at this juncture in their empire's history, and therefore were probably more inclined to respond positively to the LORD's message to them through Jonah than they otherwise might have been.

Also, M.F. Unger points out in his Introduction to the book of Jonah, that, at about the time when Jonah preached to the Ninevites, during the reign of Semiramis, the Assyrian queen regent, and her son, Adadnirari III (810-782 BC), there was 'an approach to monotheism under the god Nebo that was somewhat comparable to the earlier reforms of Amenophis IV in Egypt', and he suggests that Jonah appeared in Nineveh either in the closing years of that reign, or early in the reign of Assurdan III (771-754 BC). He further points out that Assyrian history records plagues in 765 and 759 BC, and a total eclipse of the sun in 763 BC, all of which events could have prepared the Ninevites for Jonah's message of judgement. Again, a date around 760 BC is entirely possible.

Its Outline

We here present three different outlines of differing complexity, but all of which follow the basic structure of the four chapters of the book. Here we should note that, in the Hebrew Bible, the last verse of chapter 1 in our English Bibles is made the first verse of chapter 2. There are similar slightly different chapter divisions throughout the Hebrew Bible.

Introduction to the Book of Jonah

The first outline given is the relatively brief one given by J.M. Flanigan in his commentary in the *Ritchie Old Testament What the Bible Teaches* volume which covers Daniel and the first six Minor Prophets, as follows:

Outline of the Book of Jonah

Chapter 1. Jonah's Disobedience and the Disaster
Chapter 2. Jonah's Peril and his Prayer
Chapter 3. Jonah's Recovery and Nineveh's Repentance
Chapter 4. Jonah's Displeasure and Jehovah's Decision

Secondly, this is the graphic outline given in the *King James Study Bible*:

Outline of Jonah

i   Jonah in disobedience: from the presence of the Lord to the belly of the great fish   1:1-17
   A. Jonah in the presence of God   1:1-3
   B. Jonah in the hold of the ship   1:4-9
   C. Jonah in the midst of confusion   1:10-14
   D. Jonah in the midst of the sea   1:15-16
   E. Jonah in the stomach of the fish   1:17

ii.   Jonah in repentance: from the belly of the great fish to dry land   2:1-10
   A. Jonah in prayer   2:1-9
   B. Jonah in transit   2:10

iii.   Jonah in obedience: from the dry land to Nineveh   3:1-10
   A. Jonah in fellowship with God   3: 1-4
   B. Jonah in success   3:5-9
   C. Jonah in awe   3:10

iv.   Jonah in anger: from Nineveh to the shade of the plant   4:1-11
   A. Jonah in discouragement/displeasure   4: 1-4
   B. Jonah in discomfort   4: 5-8
   C. Jonah in rebuke   4: 9-11

Thirdly, we give the instructive outline by M.F. Unger in his *Commentary on the Old Testament,* thus:

OUTLINE OF THE BOOK OF JONAH

i.	JONAH'S FIRST COMMISSION AND DISOBEDIENCE.	1: 1-17.
	A. The Lord's Commission Given and Rejected	1: 1-3.
	B. The Storm and the Sailors.	1: 4-14.
	C. Jonah Thrown Overboard and Swallowed by the Fish	1: 15-17.
ii.	JONAH'S PRAYER FROM THE FISH'S BELLY.	2: 1-10.
	A. Jonah's Cry and Travail.	2: 1-6.
	B. Jonah's Prayer, Vow, and Deliverance.	2: 7-10.
iii.	JONAH'S SECOND COMMISSION AND OBEDIENCE.	3: 1-10.
	A. Jonah's Obedience.	3: 1-4.
	B. The Ninevites Repent and Their Judgment is Withheld.	3: 5-10.
iv.	JONAH'S REACTION TO THE REVIVAL.	4: 1-11.
	A. Jonah's Displeasure and the Lord's Rebuke.	4: 1-5.
	B. Jonah Prepared for and Taught the Lord's Lesson.	4: 6-11.

Its Liturgical Use by the Jews

To this day the Book of Jonah is read by the Jews in their synagogues as the *Haphtarah,* that is, the reading from the Prophets, for the afternoon service of *Yom Kippur,* the Day of Atonement. Apparently, according to J.M. Flanigan, the reason why this book has been chosen for this most important day in the Jewish Calendar is that it exemplifies repentance and forgiveness. These essential spiritual characteristics are seen here very clearly, both in the experience of the wicked Gentile Ninevites and in the LORD's dealings with His disobedient servant Jonah.

Introduction to the Book of Jonah

Its Prophetic and Typical Significance

First, Jonah's disobedient career foreshadowed the subsequent history of his nation, Israel, in a remarkable way. Chosen as the LORD's special people from the time of the patriarchs, Israel had always been meant to witness to all the other nations concerning the uniqueness and glory of their covenant-keeping LORD God, and to become the source of blessing to them also. Sadly, they signally failed in their intended missionary commission, and determined to keep all their great privileges to themselves, rather than becoming the LORD's channel of blessing to the whole world. They have twice been scattered among the Gentile nations: first, to cure them of gross idolatry before the two Old Testament exiles in Assyria and Babylon; secondly, after they had crucified their long-awaited Messiah, the Lord Jesus Christ, and then had become a nation devoted to commercial activities, rather than to spiritual ambitions. Like Jonah, Israel have been thrown into the confused sea of the nations in the so-called *Diaspora*, the Dispersion, for their sins, but have remained distinct from them throughout over two millennia. This has caused them much persecution, but God has miraculously preserved them, like Jonah, from complete annihilation, and they have reappeared today in their own land in preparation for their part in the end time events prophesied in Scripture. Then a believing remnant of them will become ardent missionaries to all nations, both during the approaching Tribulation, then during Christ's Millennial Kingdom, a great source of blessing to the whole world, as they were originally intended to be. They will eventually repent with bitter sorrow when they witness the Christ whom they pierced at Calvary coming back in glory to deliver them from imminent destruction at the end of the Great Tribulation. The short book of Jonah beautifully typifies the main features of their history until now and in the foreseeable future.

Secondly, Jonah in his experience of being swallowed by the great fish and being inside it for three days and three nights, before being vomited up again on to the shore, typifies Christ in His death, burial, and resurrection after three days and three nights in the heart of the earth. The Lord Jesus Himself affirms this remarkable type in His dispute with the Pharisees in both Matthew chapter 12 verses 38-41 and Luke chapter 11 verses 29-

32. He claimed to be a greater than Jonah, but the leaders of the Jewish nation then failed to recognise Him for who He really is. The Lord Jesus acknowledged that Jonah was great in his preaching, because his short message of judgement upon Nineveh led to the whole city repenting and believing him. The Jews of the Lord's day were worse than the Ninevites, because they failed to repent at the preaching of Christ, unlike the Ninevites in Jonah's day, and so will face a more severe judgement than will they. Jonah in his recorded history in his book stands as a warning sign to his wayward nation, Israel. Thus we see Christ in the Book of Jonah.

Its Searching Spiritual Message for us today

This little Book of Jonah teaches us many important spiritual lessons. Some of these we will point out as we go through the following concise commentary on the narrative, but a few should be highlighted here.

First of all, we see in this book a very balanced presentation of the true character and ways of God with mankind, a perfect balance between His grace and His truth, both His holy wrath and His love and mercy. Although Jonah was sent to the wicked Ninevites with a stern message of imminent judgement from God, God's true motive in declaring this to them is revealed clearly when they repent and change their behaviour. He then has tender compassion and pity on them, and even on their little ones and cattle. He really wanted to bless them all along, but could not because of their utter wickedness. So often in the Prophets the LORD pleaded with both His people Israel and other nations to 'repent and live', so that He could bless them, but usually they stubbornly refused to do so. Jonah was sent, quite unwillingly at first, as the LORD's missionary to perhaps the most wicked nation on earth at that time, Israel's chief enemy and potential invader, and was completely successful in that they immediately repented and turned to the LORD. The result was that the Assyrian invasion of Israel was probably delayed for some years, until a later generation of Assyrians reverted to their former wicked ways. Thus we see in the book of Jonah both the goodness and the severity of God with all of us, according to our attitude and behaviour towards Him and others.

Introduction to the Book of Jonah

This perfect balance is also seen here in the LORD's dealings with His disobedient servant Jonah. First, the LORD disciplined him providentially until he repented in the belly of the great fish; then He graciously renewed His commission to him, giving him a second chance to obey His will. Secondly, when Jonah reacted to the repentance of the Ninevites with anger and complete lack of forgiveness, the LORD again used providential means in disciplining him and teaching him 'the way of God more accurately' than Jonah had understood before. He first, in grace, made a gourd to shield Jonah from the heat, but then, in discipline, made a worm and a sultry east wind to remove his temporary comfort zone, before gently remonstrating with him concerning his unforgiving attitude towards the repentant Ninevites. Yet, the very existence of this book of Jonah in Scripture probably means that Jonah did learn his lessons and repent.

However, do we see ourselves here in this autobiography of Jonah? How have we always reacted to the LORD's word to us? Have we always obeyed Him immediately and completely? Is there anything that we have stubbornly refused to do for our LORD, so that He has had to discipline us with unpleasant experiences until we did repent and obey Him? Has the LORD ever given us a second chance to obey Him, and then blessed us abundantly? Further, is there anyone whom we would rather see judged eternally than be saved through our witness, perhaps because of some wrong they have done us? Are we unforgiving, like Jonah here, for whatever reason, even after that person has repented? These are very personal and practical searching questions that arise from the study of this short prophecy. Does it almost prophesy and mirror our own spiritual history through life? How much of our God's perfectly balanced character have we both understood and reflected in our own lives and witness? Are we equally kind, but firm, with all around us, both in the assembly and the world, a model of grace and truth like the Lord Jesus Himself? This is the main challenge and searching message of the book of Jonah. Let us rise to it!

Concise Commentary on the Book of Jonah

Jonah Chapter 1

1. Jonah is commissioned to go and preach a message of judgement to the city of Nineveh, but immediately flees from the presence of the LORD towards Tarshish, effectively renouncing his prophetic office, vv. 1-3.

The book of Jonah begins with the Hebrew word for 'and'. This links the book with a long succession of Hebrew prophets to whom 'the word of the LORD' also 'came'. This phrase, which emphasises the divine nature of the message which follows, occurs about ninety times in the Old Testament, most frequently in the prophecies of Jeremiah and Ezekiel, but many times elsewhere in connection with various believers.

We have already commented on the meanings of the names 'Jonah' and 'Amittai', that they mean 'dove' and 'truthful', respectively. This suggests a balance between grace and peace, on the one hand, and truth, on the other, which, as we have seen, was sadly lacking in Jonah's life and ministry at first. Perhaps, by the time he wrote this book he had become a model of grace and truth, like his LORD God. We do trust so. M.F. Unger also suggests that the name 'dove' could indicate Jonah's 'mourning love' for his nation of Israel as they faced their surrounding Gentile enemies, such as the aggressive Assyrians. The dove is also a very clean bird, just as Jonah probably thought of himself as very ceremonially clean and distinct from the unclean nations around his people Israel. At all events, this book proves that he was an ardent nationalist, and a hawk who, at first, wished only judgement upon Israel's enemies.

In verse 2, the LORD issues Jonah with His commission to arise, and go to the great city of Nineveh in the heart of Israel's worst enemy's empire, and cry out against it, because their wickedness had so offended Him that He must soon summarily judge it. From chapter 3 we learn the substance of the LORD's message to the Assyrians then, and it may not have been much different here. Similarly, the wickedness of Sodom and Gomorrah had so offended the LORD in Abraham's days that He had had to destroy these two cities with fire and brimstone, saving 'just Lot' and his two daughters from the overthrow. Today conditions in our contemporary world are becoming very similar to those which pertained in the days of both Noah and Lot, and Scripture predicts that soon the LORD will intervene again in summary judgement to punish wicked and rebellious mankind for their mounting sins against His holiness. Both the annals of the Assyrian kings and the records within Scripture contain enough evidence to justify the LORD's decision to send a prophet to warn them of similar imminent judgement. The Assyrians were noted for gross immorality, idolatry, cruelty, and pride, and were clearly ripe for judgement. Nineveh, originally founded by Nimrod, the first great rebel against the LORD, hunter of men, and empire-builder in Genesis chapter 10, was certainly a great city in the world of that day, one of the royal residences of the Assyrian kings, and, later under Sennacherib, became the capital of the empire. Yet all great cities in the present world become centres of wickedness and vice. Nineveh was one of the worst in the ancient world, and Israel's most dangerous enemy at that time.

Why, then, according to verse 3, did Jonah react to this commission in the way he did, immediately deciding to flee in the opposite direction from Nineveh to Tarshish in either Spain or Sardinia, the far west, not the far east? Surely, he would have welcomed an opportunity to condemn Israel's worst enemy to imminent destruction. To find the answer to this problem we need to read Jonah's reaction to Nineveh's later repentance in chapter 4 verse 2. There Jonah complains bitterly to the LORD that he had previously said to Him that, if he obeyed this commission, the Ninevites would repent, and then, because he knew that the LORD was very gracious and merciful, he feared that the LORD would relent of His decision to judge Nineveh. Thus Israel would still be faced with the threat of invasion by the dreaded Assyrians. In other words, Jonah did not want the LORD to give the Assyrians any warning concerning the coming judgement, but rather to judge them without warning and opportunity to repent. So great was his hatred of Israel's national enemies that he just wanted them to be destroyed eternally. However, it is a principle with God that He rarely judges anyone without first warning them of the judgement coming, so that they might repent and be saved from disaster. Jonah understood some of the LORD's character accurately, but had a deficient view of it, so that he ignored some essential aspects of His ways with mankind. He learned more later; but have we? Is there anyone whom we would prefer to be condemned eternally, rather than to be saved? Are we also as unforgiving as this? Yet our Lord is not like this at all. He prayed for His enemies as they were crucifying Him, that His Father would forgive them, because they did not know what they were doing. Often, our enemies who persecute us seriously misunderstand us, and sincerely believe that they must do the wrong things that they are doing to us; even, that God wants them to kill us as part of serving Him. However, here the ancient Assyrians were probably motivated more by political ambition and national pride in themselves than a misguided desire to persecute the people of God, which was pure greed and selfishness. At all events, Jonah was not prepared to become party to giving his people's enemies any opportunity to repent and escape the LORD's summary judgement.

In verse 3, the twice repeated phrase that Jonah was attempting to flee 'from the presence of the LORD' probably means that he was attempting to renounce his office as a prophet of the LORD, because he felt that he could no longer fulfil the LORD's commissions to him. He probably did not think that he could ever find a place where the LORD was not present, since he would have believed the Old Testament Scriptures, such as Psalm 139, which speak of the omnipresence of God very clearly. Has the LORD ever told us to do something which we feel we cannot do, or do not wish to do, for Him? Have we ever been 'disobedient to the heavenly vision', like Jonah here?

At first, all seemed to go smoothly for Jonah in his chosen path of disobedience. When he arrived at the seaport of Joppa, which was later known as Jaffa, and is located just south of modern-day Tel-Aviv, he quite easily found a ship that was going to Tarshish, and was able to pay the right fare and go on board at once. However, an easy pathway is not necessarily a sign that God approves of our movements in life, since it may be directly contrary to His Word, as Jonah's pathway was here. Sometimes God's right way for us is the most difficult pathway that we could imagine, but He promises to be with us throughout it. Note that the book says that every step Jonah took at this stage was 'down', right into the sides of the ship's hold, in a spiritual as well as a physical sense. Was he going to get away with his disobedience and to be able to start a new life far away from his homeland? Do you really think that we will be able to do this in our own day and circumstances?

2. The LORD, in disciplining His disobedient servant, hurls a great tempest on the sea, threatening the safety of all on board the ship, so that the captain interrogated Jonah to find out the reason why this had happened, and Jonah had to confess that he was the cause of the crisis, and then told the sailors to throw him overboard, vv. 4-12.

Now God will never stand idly by when His servants so deliberately disobey His clear commands. He will discipline them until they repent. This is only evidence of His Fatherly love for us, and it is intended for our good; see Hebrews chapter 12. Accordingly, after Jonah had attempted to renounce his prophetic office by fleeing 'from the presence of the LORD', which is an impossible thing to do, the LORD 'hurled a great wind into the sea', which caused a great tempest to arise, threatening to wreck the ship. Even the seasoned mariners recognised that this was a supernatural storm, and cried out to their various pagan gods for help. They threw out the ship's cargo into the sea to lighten the ship, and wondered what else they could do. They were rather annoyed to find that Jonah was lying fast asleep in the sides of the ship's hold while the tempest was raging, quite oblivious to the danger into which he had brought the whole company. The ship's captain rudely awoke Jonah, and asked him why he was not helping to save their lives by calling on his God also. The crew decided to cast lots to find out the culprit, since they suspected that someone on board had committed some crime which had merited this catastrophe, and the lot fell on Jonah, by the LORD's providential guidance. This was another miracle; see Proverbs 16. 33. By cross-questioning Jonah, the sailors found out the whole truth of the situation. Jonah was a Hebrew who feared the LORD God of heaven, earth, and sea, and yet had fled from the presence of the LORD for some reason. We do not know if he told the sailors about his commission to Nineveh, and its precise import, but he may well have done so, since he was compelled to become very honest with these unfortunate pagans. They acted throughout this distressing scene most honourably, unlike Jonah. Sadly, sometimes men of the world behave better than the LORD's own people. They asked Jonah as a man of God what they should do to him to save the situation. He, in his turn, bravely told them to throw him overboard. He knew that, if they did so, the sea would at once become calm again. He made a full confession of the fact that he was the cause of all their trouble, and was prepared to lose his own life to save theirs; this was very commendable. Jonah wanted to die, rather than fulfil his commission from the LORD.

3. At first, the sailors tried hard to row the ship to land, but when they realised they could not, they prayed that the LORD would not condemn them for obeying Jonah's instruction, then threw him overboard into the sea, which immediately became calm; but the LORD intervened to save Jonah by preparing a great fish to swallow him, and he was in the fish for three days and three nights, vv 13-17.

We must give these heathen sailors full credit for doing all in their power to avoid throwing Jonah overboard. They rowed really hard to try to bring the ship to land, but they eventually found that they could not, because the LORD caused the sea to become more and more tempestuous. When they could do no more, they cried out to the LORD, Jonah's professed God, not to let them perish because they had had to, as they thought, let him drown in the sea, and fully acknowledged what they clearly understood to be the LORD's will in the matter. So they picked up Jonah, and hurled him into the sea, which immediately stopped raging and became quite calm. The whole incident had such a profound effect on them that they feared the LORD greatly, offered a sacrifice, probably one of thanksgiving for their deliverance from death, and made vows to the LORD, presumably to live differently and to worship Him, rather than their former heathen idols. We are not given any clear details concerning this, but they may well have come to trust in the LORD personally, and to experience His salvation. This was really in spite of Jonah's bad testimony at the time, and not because of it. God is so great that He can use us in His purposes of grace even in spite of our sometimes poor testimony.

Finally, we should note again what was indicated in the Introduction, that verse 17 in our English Bibles is actually verse 1 of chapter 2 in the Hebrew Bible. It is a bridge verse, concluding the traumatic events of chapter 1, and preparing the way for Jonah's very genuine prayer of repentance and anticipation of salvation from death in chapter 2. It records another remarkable miracle, the preparation by the LORD of a great fish to swallow down Jonah as he was hurled by the sailors into the sea, and thus to keep him safe in its stomach for three days and three nights, until he was ejected from it on to the shore of the land from which he had set sail.

The Lord Jesus quoted this verse in His rebuke of His enemies, the Jewish religious leaders, in Matthew chapter 12 and Luke chapter 11, in order to assert that what happened to Jonah for three days and three nights in the belly of the great fish was a sign to them of what would soon happen to Himself, when, after His crucifixion and death, He was buried for three days and three nights in the heart of the earth. Jonah was a sign to the Ninevites, and they all repented at his preaching. The Lord Jesus was a sign to the generation of Israel who heard His preaching, and who signally failed to repent and believe on Him, a sign, presumably, of coming inevitable judgement for their sins and rejection of Himself, the Incarnate Son of God. Then the Lord Jesus claimed to be greater than Jonah, making the nation's rejection of Him the more culpable.

The three days and three nights mentioned here are to be understood according to the Jewish method of reckoning, not ours, which would take them as three whole days and three whole nights. Actually, the Lord Jesus was buried for part of the Friday and part of the first day of the week, and was only in the grave for the whole of the Sabbath, the Saturday, but the Jews regarded any part of a day or night as a full day or night. Hence the three days and three nights are perfectly accurate, and not a mistake. Here in Jonah, the three days and three nights may have been similarly somewhat shorter than the full extent of three whole days and three whole nights, although we cannot be sure about that.

Jonah Chapter 2

Jonah's poetic prayer to the LORD his God out of the fish's stomach in three movements, each beginning with a rehearsal of his impossible circumstances, but concluding with a clear statement of his faith in God to save him, until the LORD spoke to the fish, so that it vomited Jonah on to the dry land, vv. 1-10.

The great fish both protected Jonah from harm in the sea, and disciplined him further, since he could not naturally see any way out of his predicament. It is not unknown for seamen to be swallowed by a great fish, such as a sperm whale, and to survive until they were rescued some time later. The story is true to real life, not a myth, as unbelievers have thought.

This is the first time in the book that Jonah is said to pray to the LORD his God. Note that he says 'his God', whom he really knew before, but with whom he had been sadly out of communion for some time now. It took a real crisis and an impossible predicament to prompt Jonah to renew his prayer life with the LORD. By contrast, as believers, we should pray at all times, and not just when we are in great distress. God is not just an insurance policy for desperate emergencies, although He is our only Helper then, but wants to be our constant Companion through life, and our sovereign Lord directing our lives always.

Jonah's prayer was clearly written after he had been delivered from the virtual tomb of the great fish's belly, and is composed in good Hebrew poetry. It has three movements, all of which follow a similar thought pattern. First, he states his predicament, then he expresses his genuine faith in the LORD to deliver him. The three sections are as follows: verses 2-4; verses 5-6; verses 7-9. This prayer reveals that Jonah had a good knowledge of Scripture, especially the Psalms, although he only quoted short extracts from many of them. His mind was saturated with Scripture, but his life was not being lived fully in accordance with it. Is there a similar gap between our doctrine and our daily practice, as there was here with Jonah? This is the way to become a hypocrite, and the laughing-stock of the world around us. Beware, believer! Be consistent with your faith!

In verses 2-4, Jonah acknowledges that, when he called out in his distress to the LORD, He answered him. He cried for help from what must have seemed to be the depths of Sheol, and the LORD hearkened to his voice, although he had rejected the LORD's commission previously. What grace to an erring saint! His experience as he had been thrown into the sea, when the currents engulfed him, so that the waves went over his body, had been terrible, but now he saw that it had been the LORD who had cast him there to teach him a needed lesson of obedience. He felt that he had been expelled from the LORD's sight as a reprobate servant. However, he now determined once more to look in faith towards the LORD's holy temple in Jerusalem, the only true centre of Israel's worship, the place where the LORD's Glory-cloud of His presence dwelt, and the only source of help for himself now. Would he ever see it again? Perhaps Jonah still really believed that he would do so. His faith begins to shine through his tears of anguish.

Then, in verses 5-6, Jonah continues to express his feelings as he sank into the sea and was swallowed by the fish. He thought that he was going to die by drowning, as the deep waters of the Mediterranean engulfed him, and he felt weeds around his head, perhaps literally, even as he was being swallowed into the fish's stomach. He seemed to be going down and down to the bottoms of the mountains, and he felt like a prisoner trapped in a dungeon forever. Yet then he acknowledged that the LORD his God, who had allowed all this to happen to him as chastisement for his sin of disobedience, had later brought up his life from the watery grave around him. Praise His Name!

Finally, in verses 7-9, Jonah remembers how the LORD had listened to his despairing prayer, and saved him as he had been losing all hope of deliverance, and possibly literally fainting as a result of his incarceration inside the darkness of the fish's stomach. He realised as never before that the LORD, from whom he was so foolishly fleeing, was his only, but sure, hope, and his earnest prayer for help had reached Him in His holy temple. Jonah knew that the LORD was too great to dwell only in magnificent temples made with hands, as Solomon had said on the day of the dedication of the Jerusalem temple so long before. No, God is everywhere available to hear his repentant saints' cries. He is the only true God, and Jonah knew this very well, and said that those who worship worthless and futile idols forsake their own mercy, which they could have found in the LORD God of Israel. Jonah remembered that the sailors had been quite unable to help him or themselves by calling on their various idolatrous gods, and he now determined, repentantly, to sacrifice to the LORD his God and express his sincere thanksgiving to Him, because he had experienced personally the truth of the verse which asserts that 'Salvation is of the LORD'. He now promised to pay his vow made to the LORD for rescuing him from death by drowning or suffocation, and determined to repent of his former disobedience in refusing to go to preach the LORD's message of judgement to the city of Nineveh.

The LORD's discipline of His wayward servant was beginning to bear fruit, so now He spoke to the fish, and the fish vomited Jonah back on to the dry land where he had started from. However, as we shall find later in chapter 4, Jonah still had some further major lessons to learn from God. While his good knowledge of Scripture and his personal faith in the LORD had enabled him to survive his ordeal and experience deliverance, he still needed more humility, self-judgement, and compassion in his dealings with others around him, especially the poor, benighted Assyrians, to whom the LORD had commissioned him to go. The LORD's lesson to Jonah was only half-finished.

Also, consider how much easier it would have been for Jonah, if he had obeyed the word of the LORD to him the first time he heard it. He had wasted precious time intended to be used for his God. Have we ever done this? The LORD in grace had brought

Jonah back to the same land from which he had started. Now He could re-commission him for the greatest mission of his prophetic ministry. Remember how, in Genesis chapter 13, the LORD had brought Abram back from his wandering down into Egypt, sadly rebuked by an ungodly Pharaoh and cluttered with Egyptian baggage, to the same place from which he had set out, and to the same altar at Bethel. The LORD will, if necessary, do the same with us, if we wander away from Him, but, when we repent under His disciplining hand, He will enable us to make a fresh start in life and in His service. How longsuffering and gracious the LORD is with all of us! Hallelujah!

Jonah Chapter 3

1. The LORD's second commission to Jonah to go to preach at Nineveh, giving him a second chance to obey Him, followed by the account of Jonah's journey there, and his brief message of judgement, vv. 1-4.

Now the word of the LORD came to Jonah the second time. How very gracious the LORD was to give Jonah a second chance to obey Him! He did not discard him, and call another (more obedient) servant, but, having chastised him severely in the great fish, He simply called Jonah again, giving him a message to preach that was very similar to the one He had given him previously in chapter 1. Probably, many of us can testify to the fact that God has sometimes given us second chances to do His will in various respects, perhaps even more opportunities than this. He is very longsuffering with His children, and we are such slow and unwilling disciples of His. Failure need not be final, if only we are prepared to humble ourselves under His mighty disciplining hand and to obey Him the second, or perhaps the third, time around. Usually, only often-repeated disobedience and sheer stubbornness end in summary judgement and final disaster. Therefore, one further lesson for us today is that we should, like the Lord our Master, be very patient with those whom He has entrusted to our care and teaching. They, like us, will often be very slow learners, and sometimes fail to follow our example of obedience to the Lord, but we should persevere graciously with them, until they do respond to the word of God positively. Here Jonah is said to have obeyed his second summons implicitly and immediately.

According to verse 2, it would appear that, when Jonah set out to travel to Nineveh, which was about five hundred miles east - north-east of Israel, he did not yet know precisely what the LORD's message to that wicked city was going to be, since the LORD said that He was going to tell him this nearer the time of his arrival there. However, by the time he did reach the city he evidently did know exactly what to proclaim to its citizens. Nineveh was one of the greatest and largest cities in the ancient world at that time. In fact, verse 3 literally says, in the original Hebrew, that Nineveh was a 'great city to God'. Apparently, the mind of the Hebrews associated all greatness with God, regardless of the spiritual condition of those people or things that were so described. When archaeologists began, in the mid-nineteenth century, to excavate the ruins of Nineveh, which had lain beneath the surface of the land for many centuries undiscovered, so that some unbelievers doubted that it had ever existed historically, they found that it was a vast metropolitan conurbation with many suburbs, wide streets and walls, and impressive buildings and hanging gardens covering a wide area, certainly requiring at least three days to walk through its full area, as Jonah began to do. Assyriology has become a well-researched area of ancient history, supported by a vast cuneiform literature on clay tablets, which is still being studied today. The more material the archaeologists find in their excavations, the more it tends to confirm the truth and accuracy of the Biblical record. God's word is true from the beginning to the end! Not that our simple faith depends on such evidence, but this does confirm the accuracy of the Bible to rank unbelievers.

Verse 4 says that Jonah began to walk through the city for one day, perhaps winding about through all the streets to cover all areas of it, rather than taking a straight line through it from one end to the other. As he walked through, he was constantly proclaiming the LORD's brief message of judgement as a serious warning to the wicked citizens, saying, 'In forty days' time, Nineveh will be overthrown', that is, supernaturally, like Sodom and Gomorrah, because of its extreme wickedness. This message seems to be an advance on the one that the LORD told him to proclaim in chapter 1, since there the LORD simply told him to cry against it because of its wickedness, but said nothing about an imminent overthrow after forty days. God's summary judgement was hanging over the Ninevites like the sword of Damocles. What would be the reaction of this wicked pagan city, the devotees of the idolatrous fish god,

Dagon, to the preaching of the strange man who had survived being swallowed by a great fish? Would the authorities there arrest Jonah forthwith and kill him for preaching a 'hate message', as could easily happen to open-air preachers in our own cities today? It must have taken considerable courage for Jonah to fulfil his commission, but fulfil it he did, quite faithfully, and waited for the response.

2. The Ninevites repented, believed in God, and called on Him earnestly to help them to turn from their wicked ways, with the result that He relented of His purposed judgement, and spared them from the threatened calamity, vv. 5-10.

Amazingly, the Ninevites immediately believed in the message which Jonah was preaching from God, and also gave evidence of genuine repentance by covering themselves with sackcloth and ashes as a sign of deep mourning for their sins. This was a remarkable miracle of grace which could not really have been foreseen, although we have, in the Introduction to this Book of Jonah, given several good reasons to believe that the Assyrians of that generation had been providentially prepared to accept the ministry of a Hebrew prophet like Jonah rather more easily than generations either before, or after, this one. Certainly, later generations of Assyrians did revert to their old wicked ways, and both Micah and Nahum had to prophesy severely against them at a somewhat later date. By contrast, Jonah's generation gave proof of their true repentance by calling upon God in earnest prayer for His help in changing their wicked behaviour to accord with His holiness. Even the king of Nineveh, who may have been either the emperor of all Assyria, or perhaps the local city ruler delegated by the latter, joined wholeheartedly in the general spirit of repentance and conversion, and called on his people to observe a general strict fast in the emergency. Even their animals were involved in this fast and covering with sackcloth, so earnest were they in their pleas for salvation from disaster.

We seriously wonder what comparable effect such a preaching of imminent summary judgement would have on citizens in our countries today. Yet in the weekly proclamation of the gospel throughout our lands there is really just such a stark warning of doom and disaster for those who reject the word of the LORD through the servants of God. We suspect a great deal of apathy and actual opposition would meet the preachers of doomsday today. Many would not believe that the judgement would ever come, and laugh at the servants of God. Certainly, most people today do not accept the message of life and salvation, nor consider that it is necessary because of our original sin. Only a minority believe the Bible at all. Yet it is being gradually proved true by many events happening around us today, if only unbelievers had eyes to see them. Sadly, they are blinded by the god of this age from receiving the light of the gospel of the glory of God in the face of Jesus Christ.

We should note here the amazing fact that Jonah, probably the most disobedient of the LORD's prophets, was also by far the most successful of them in his preaching. Almost all the Old Testament prophets had very few, if any, converts or disciples, but Jonah's preaching, under the power of the Spirit of God, was responsible for the conversion of a whole enemy city. This tells us the very sobering lesson, that success in preaching does not always indicate the godliness of the preacher. God can work in spite of us, as well as through us; He is sovereign at all times. What He values in us, first and foremost, is utter faithfulness to His word, and implicit and immediate obedience.

Thus, the Ninevites had cast themselves entirely on God's mercy, acknowledging their wickedness. God responded, as He always does to such humble repentance and faith, by relenting of the evil that He had said He would do to them, and He did not execute judgement against Nineveh at that time. In fact, there was a stay of execution for the whole Assyrian Empire for about another 150 years, until 612 BC. Then it was left to the prophet Nahum to announce Nineveh's final doom at the hands of the Babylonians. God's mercy rejoices against His judgement, for judgement is God's 'strange work'; see Isaiah 28. 21. Lamentations chapter 3 verse 33 says that 'He doth not afflict willingly nor grieve the children of men', since He takes account of our extreme frailty as creatures of dust. However, had Jonah learned this lesson yet?

Jonah Chapter 4

1. Jonah became very angry that the LORD had relented of His purpose to judge the Ninevites, since they were Israel's worst enemies, reminding the LORD that he had feared all along that this would happen, and therefore had refused to obey the LORD's first commission; and then he asked the LORD to take his life from him, but the LORD questioned whether Jonah was right to be angry with Him, vv. 1-4.

Jonah's story now moves to a climax in the wayward prophet's serious confrontation with the LORD Himself over His decision not to condemn Nineveh at that time in view of their repentance. Here Jonah learns his final and most important lessons concerning his God, and the essential spirit in which he should serve Him.

Jonah had not been at all taken by surprise by this turn of events, for he was well aware of the LORD's gracious and merciful character. In fact, he was, wrongly, very displeased with the LORD, and became very angry with Him. His audacity in the situation is very sad, as he virtually told the Almighty, 'There You are, I told You so!' May the LORD keep us from doing the same when we do not appreciate His dealings with us! Jonah was angry, because the LORD's grace to the Ninevites meant that the Assyrian enemies of Israel were not going to be destroyed after all. Nineveh was being given a second chance to become obedient to God, just as the LORD had given Jonah himself a second chance to obey Him. Perhaps the disgruntled prophet conveniently ignored that fact, thus revealing his selfishness and narrow-minded nationalism. He so hated the Assyrians that he just wanted them to be eliminated from the world scene. Also, he may well have resented the fact that the LORD had allowed him to look somewhat foolish, because his message of judgement had not been fulfilled. That was the real reason why he had fled to go to Tarshish in the first place, renouncing his prophetic ministry. So twice in this chapter Jonah asks the LORD to take his life from him, for without an effective ministry, so he thought, his life was no longer worth living.

Clearly, therefore, although Jonah in one sense knew the LORD's character of grace as well as justice, in another sense he completely failed to appreciate it in all its wonder and loveliness. God's love is made known to the completely unworthy and unlovely, such as all of us are by nature. That is the essential nature of God, and we need to realise that, if we are to understand all His ways with us. Jonah should have rejoiced over open sinners repenting in Nineveh, just as the LORD does today, and all the angels of heaven with Him. Jonah was really very like the elder brother in Luke chapter 15 who resented all the 'fuss' being made of his wayward younger brother when he did eventually come home to his father. Yet are we today in any way like him? Are we ready to forgive those who trespass against us, when they turn to us in repentance? Is there anyone known to us now whom we would really not wish to be saved and delivered from eternal judgement? Are we hard, unforgiving, and self-centred, like Jonah here?

The LORD could not rightly allow His angry servant to go unchallenged and undisciplined after this unholy outburst. It would not have been kind to him to do so. Jonah must learn more of his God's ways and character in practice, as we need to also, for we shall all meet Him one day and be judged by Him for reward or loss of reward. Failure to judge ourselves now will result in eternal loss of reward then. Accordingly, the remainder of the chapter, and of the whole book, concerns the LORD's correction of Jonah by disciplinary measures.

2. When Jonah went out of the city of Nineveh and sat down to see what would happen to it, the LORD first prepared a plant to give Jonah shade from the sun, but then prepared a worm to attack the plant, so that it withered, and also a scorching east wind to make Jonah feel faint in the heat, so that he asked again to die, vv. 5-8.
Jonah went out of the city of Nineveh on its east side, made

himself a booth, or tent of tree branches and leaves, and sat under it in the shade to see whether the LORD would change His mind concerning the fate of Nineveh and destroy it, or not. He seemingly could not understand why Israel's chief enemy at that time was being spared the summary judgement that he had been instrumental in announcing against it. His heart was not yet in sympathy with the LORD's concerning the heathen nations around his own people Israel.

Therefore, the LORD proceeded to prepare, or appoint, three things, in order to teach Jonah a needed lesson about his unfortunate attitude to the lost nations around him. First, he appointed a gourd, or plant (the exact meaning of its name is not known with certainty), which grew up miraculously quickly to provide Jonah with needed shade from the sun. Jonah was very happy with this divine provision, since it allowed him to stay within his comfort zone as he watched events around Nineveh, rather selfishly. Next day, at dawn, God appointed a worm to attack the plant, so that it withered away, and ceased to shield Jonah from the sun. Then, when the sun rose, God further appointed a vehement, scorching, east wind, which caused the sun to beat down on Jonah's defenceless head, until he became faint, and again asked to die, because death seemed to him better than continuing to live under such adverse conditions. Jonah was consumed with self-centred anger again. He seemed only to be thinking of how this situation affected him and his own people Israel, not how the LORD really thought about the Ninevites, who had clearly repented of their wickedness. M.F. Unger writes concerning this paragraph detailing God's dealings with His servant, 'The LORD had taken away the creature comforts of which Jonah was so joyously solicitous, and in their place imposed severe discomforts. That disciplinary dealing was a necessary prelude to getting the attention of the self-dominated prophet in order to teach him the lesson of surrender to God's will in selfless service in behalf of (that is, on behalf of) lost humanity worldwide'. Jonah was now overcome by severe spiritual depression, but was also ready to listen to the LORD's much-needed lesson concerning the withered gourd, or plant, that was here used as a parable of His dealings with the repentant Ninevites.

3. ***The LORD challenges Jonah to consider whether he was right to be angry about the demise of the gourd, and when Jonah stubbornly insists that he was, the LORD rebukes Jonah for being grieved about the plant, for which he had done nothing, but not sharing His own compassion for the citizens of the great city of Nineveh, many of whom were not fully morally responsible for their actions, but had repented as a result of Jonah's preaching, vv. 9-11.***

Again, God quite gently asked Jonah whether, or not, he was justified in being angry with Him over the loss of the shade of the gourd. The LORD did not severely rebuke him, despite Jonah's audacity in objecting to His ways with him. Jonah, for his part, felt that he was fully justified in being angry with the LORD. Now life for him was not worth living any longer. Whatever special treatment was he expecting as the LORD's servant?

Now the LORD uses the gourd as a parable to illustrate the lesson that He knew Jonah needed to learn concerning the Ninevites. He asks Jonah an unanswerable question in the closing two verses of the book. If Jonah had compassion on the gourd, for which he had not worked, nor had caused to grow, just a worthless plant which had grown up one night and perished the next, why should not the LORD have compassion on the great city of Nineveh, in which lived more than 120,000 people who were both very vulnerable and not fully morally responsible, as well as many valuable cattle? Jonah was being very inconsistent in his priorities, because he was consumed with racial hatred against Israel's greatest enemy city at that time, and had failed to understand the loving heart of God for all His creatures without partiality or exception. All men, not just the chosen people of Israel, are infinitely precious to God, and He loves them all equally. Jonah had no compassion on the poor, ignorant, heathen Ninevites when they gave good evidence of repentance and conversion to God, but had had pity on a worthless plant like the gourd, after it perished, just because it provided him with some shade from the sun. He was being entirely selfish, and had utterly failed to appreciate the sovereign grace of God towards lost sinners like the benighted Assyrians when they repented. Jonah seems to have been silenced by this searching question, which points us to the main searching message of the whole book of Jonah, that we should love all men equally as God does, and rejoice over any indication that they are turning to Him, no matter how wicked they may have been in the past.

Therefore, finally, we should consider how far we today are in sympathy with the heart of God concerning poor sinful men and women around us. Christ died for them just as much as for us, and God loves them just as much as He loves us, although we do not always behave as if He does. God is not partial; neither should we be. Wherever people give evidence of repentance at God's word, let us hasten to forgive them and to show them love and grace, as God delights to do. In His Sermon on the Mount, the Lord Jesus gave His disciples clear instruction concerning their enemies. He said, in Matthew chapter 5 verses 43 and 44, 'You have heard that it was said, "You shall love your neighbour, and hate your enemy"', which is the Old Testament standard, 'But I say unto you, love your enemies, and pray for those who persecute you' (NASB), which is the New Testament standard. After all, we are just as much indebted to the LORD for our salvation as they are. Surely, there should be no-one whom we would not rejoice to see coming to the Saviour. However, does our lack of concern for the lost people around us betray our real feelings in the matter? May the LORD challenge us concerning this, for it affects His glory and His will in the world! We believe that Jonah did learn this lesson, although by the hard way, but have we also yet learned it? God grant that this may be true of us also!

MICAH

Micah, the Prophet who Predicted Christ's Birth and Israel's Final Salvation

Introduction to Micah's Prophecy

Its Canonical Setting

The prophecy of Micah is placed sixth in the canonical order of the twelve Minor Prophets, after the book of Jonah, and before the prophecy of Nahum. This is probably its chronological position also, since Jonah prophesied during the reign of Jeroboam II of Israel, perhaps in about 760 BC, while Nahum prophesied during the following century, shortly before the fall of Assyria to the Babylonians in 612 BC. Micah prophesied during the reigns of Jotham, Ahaz, and Hezekiah of Judah, that is, during the latter half of the eighth century BC. What is significant about these three consecutive prophets is that they all prophesied either against or concerning the Assyrians, who were at that time in Israel's history the nation's chief enemy. First, as a result of Jonah's preaching against Nineveh, the chief city of Assyria, the Assyrians repented of their sins, and were granted over a century of further prosperity. Then, later, Micah names 'the Assyrian' as the LORD's chief instrument of judgement against both Israel and Judah, during the time when Samaria was captured by the Assyrians and its citizens were deported into exile. Finally, Nahum was inspired to predict with amazing accuracy and detail the fall of Nineveh to the invading Babylonians. The Assyrian Empire was absorbed into the expanding Babylonian Empire of Nebuchadnezzar, and did not regain its former power. Its judgement then was decisive, although we do know from some of the references to 'the Assyrian' in Micah and Isaiah that this people and power will be revived in the end times, and will have a significant part to play both in the wars of the Tribulation and also in the blessings of the subsequent Millennial Kingdom of Christ. Thus, the canonical setting of this Prophecy of Micah is quite significant, and instructive.

Its Historical Background and Date

If, as Micah chapter 1 verse 1 states, Micah prophesied during the reigns of Jotham (740-736 BC), Ahaz (736-716 BC), and Hezekiah (716-687 BC), all kings of Judah, then he must have written his book during the latter half of the eighth century BC, and some scholarly believers think that most of it was written in the period from about 740 to 720 BC. However, Jeremiah quoted Micah chapter 3 verse 12 in his chapter 26 verses 17-18, and clearly stated that Micah made the prediction in that verse during the reign of Hezekiah, that is, somewhat later than 720 BC. Jeremiah also implied in his reference to him that Micah was not martyred, but probably died a natural death, unlike many other true prophets of the LORD. Perhaps he died during the latter part of good king Hezekiah's reign, in peace and unmolested by his contemporaries. Micah was probably a slightly younger contemporary of Isaiah, but may have died before him.

Now while Jotham and Hezekiah were good kings of Judah, Ahaz was thoroughly wicked, and led his people into gross idolatry and corruption, and also into a highly dangerous foreign policy of alliance with Assyria. Although Jotham was a generally good king who obeyed the LORD, he failed to remove the idolatrous high places from his kingdom, and his subjects still frequented them; see 2 Kings 15. 32-38. Hezekiah rectified both this, and the gross iniquities of his immediate predecessor, Ahaz, and was miraculously helped by the LORD to survive the Assyrian king Sennacherib's siege of Jerusalem in 701 BC, but he did make a few costly mistakes through pride in his treasures and selfishly pleading for his life during a serious illness. Many of the ordinary citizens, and some of the rulers in Judah, failed to follow the good kings' leads, and the general picture of the moral and spiritual condition of the Southern Kingdom during much of the latter half of the eighth century BC, as it is described by Micah, is very depressing. There was evidently widespread materialism, corruption, and oppression of the poor by the wealthy, and the hypocrisy, syncretism, and formality of the people's worship of the LORD was nauseating to Him. Idolatry had become the norm in Judah, especially during Ahaz's reign, and was not fully eradicated by Hezekiah's reforms.

Micah's prophecy reflects much of the highs and lows of this period of Judah's history. There are severe condemnations of sin and dire warnings of coming judgement at the hands of both Assyria and Babylon for both sectors of the Divided Kingdom, but, like his fellow-prophet Isaiah, he was also inspired to predict several important prophecies concerning Christ's birth and coming Millennial Kingdom. There are pleas for the people's repentance and assurances of the ultimate fulfilment of the LORD's unconditional promises to Abraham and the other patriarchs. Micah has been too long neglected by Bible students beside the longer books of the Major Prophets, especially that of Isaiah, which his book in many respects resembles.

Its Authorship and Main Characteristics

Not a great deal is known about the prophet Micah, except that he came from a small town in southwest Judah called Moresheth-gath in the lowlands called the Shephelah near the country of the Philistines about twenty miles from Jerusalem. He was clearly a Judaean by birth, who prophesied in Jerusalem. However, he prophesied concerning both the Northern Kingdom of Israel based on Samaria and also the Southern Kingdom of Judah during the period when the Assyrians invaded the Northern Kingdom, besieged Samaria, and eventually carried its citizens into exile in Assyria. Some verses in his prophecy seem to anticipate the Assyrian siege of Jerusalem by Sennacherib in 701 BC, but Micah does not say that Jerusalem fell then, which it did not due to the LORD's miraculous intervention, and Micah may not have lived to see this event take place, unlike Isaiah, his slightly older contemporary, who recorded it in full detail. Micah's prophecy has been called 'Isaiah in shorthand', because it contains many similarities to Isaiah's prophecy both in the nature of his messages of condemnation for sin and predictions of judgement for it, and in his subsequent predictions of Israel's ultimate restoration and glory. The prediction found in Micah chapter 4 verses 1-5 is parallel

Introduction to Micah's Prophecy

to that in Isaiah chapter 2 verses 2-4. Although it is unclear which prophet is quoting the other, some commentators think that Micah may be quoting Isaiah here. We have already referred to Micah's prophecy in chapter 3 verse 12 that Jerusalem would become a ploughed field, which Jeremiah quotes in Jeremiah chapter 26 verses 18-19 as having been made during the reign of good king Hezekiah. The fact that Micah was not condemned for making this prediction was used by some of Jeremiah's loyal contemporaries to shield Jeremiah from martyrdom. That passage probably indicates that Micah was not martyred, but died a natural death in peace sometime during Hezekiah's reign.

Micah's name means 'Who is like the LORD?', and he is to be distinguished from the earlier prophet Micaiah the son of Imlah, who, according to 1 Kings chapter 22, ministered to the wicked king Ahab of Israel during the ninth century BC. Micah was contemporary not only with Isaiah in Judah, but also with Hosea and Amos, prophets to the Northern Kingdom. Micah does not mention any kings of the Northern Kingdom of Israel, although he lived during the short reigns of many of the last of them; only prophets to Israel make mention of any kings of Israel. In the last few verses of Micah's prophecy there is a wordplay on his name, as he exclaims to the LORD, 'Who is a pardoning God like Thee?'

Like Isaiah, Micah is a prophet who preached personal and social righteousness, and he condemned the wealthy landowners in both parts of the Divided Kingdom for their heartless oppression of the poor and innocent. However, all through his short prophecy Micah interspersed sermons of condemnation and imminent judgement with glorious predictions of Israel's restoration and ultimate salvation and blessing in the end times and the Millennial Kingdom of Christ.

Its Literary Skill and Linguistic Difficulties

Micah's prophecy displays a literary skill similar to that of his fellow-prophet Isaiah, and his book is a good example of classical Hebrew poetry. However, whereas Isaiah was a court poet and historian, born into a high-ranking social circle, Micah was a lowly country rustic from an obscure village. Isaiah was a statesman of note, who advised several kings of Judah, but Micah was a social reformer and evangelist, who majored on personal piety and social morality to the ordinary citizens. They each served their respective audiences with great faithfulness. God has His true witnesses in all strata of society.

Some verses in the prophecy of Micah are difficult to understand in the original language, and it is clear that the older translators of the book have sometimes had difficulty deciding on the best rendering of them. It is therefore advisable to compare the older Authorised/King James Version of the book with a few more recent literal translations, which have benefitted from more recent believing scholarship.

Micah's book contains a number of interesting Hebrew puns, which are plays on the meaning of several Hebrew words. In particular, in chapter 7 verse 18, he ends his prophecy with a pun on the meaning of his own name, 'Who is like the LORD?', as he exclaims in adoration of God, 'Who is a God like unto Thee, that pardoneth iniquity, and passeth by the transgression of His heritage?', that is, Israel. Further, in chapter 1 verses 10-15, there is a succession of puns on the meanings of many place-names in south-west Judah which would soon be affected by the invading armies of the Assyrians in 701 BC. In the following concise commentary on chapter 1, there is an attempt to explain these and to give some examples of good translations of them, notably those by James Moffatt in his *New Translation of the Bible*, published in 1926.

Its Quotations

First of all, we have already noted the verses in Micah chapter 4 which are parallel with verses in Isaiah chapter 2 verses 2-4. Here it is perhaps more likely that Micah is quoting Isaiah, rather than that Isaiah is quoting Micah, but this is uncertain. We have also noted that, in Jeremiah chapter 26 verses 18-19, the rulers who were favourable towards Jeremiah quoted Micah's prophecy in chapter 3 verse 12 that Jerusalem would be ploughed up like a field and the LORD's temple there destroyed. They pointed out to Jeremiah's accusers of treason and sacrilege that, after Micah had made this bold prediction, he had not been martyred by the good reigning king, Hezekiah, because the latter believed the LORD's true prophets. Thus they rescued Jeremiah from his attackers and almost certain death.

Secondly, there are two quotations of Micah's prophecy in the New Testament. The prophecy in Micah chapter 5 verse 2 concerning Christ's birthplace in Bethlehem Ephratah, His lineage, and eternal origin is quoted by the Jewish chief priests and scribes to king Herod in Matthew chapter 2 verses 4-6 in answer to the latter's enquiry as to where, according to their Scriptures, the Christ was to be born. Sadly, their knowledge of the Scripture did not lead them to recognise or accept the young child Jesus as the Christ and Israel's long-awaited king, unlike the Gentile wise men, who had seen His star in the east.

Then, again in Matthew's Gospel chapter 10 verses 35-36, the Lord Jesus quoted Micah chapter 7 verse 6 when He is explaining to His twelve disciples the sad effects that His ministry would have upon those who would become His disciples. The effect of allegiance to Him would be to bring division, strife, and enmity between family members, not peace at all, as different members took different standpoints in relation to His claims upon them. Some would accept and believe Him, whereas others certainly would not, and would persecute those who did follow Him. In Micah chapter 7, the prophet is simply bemoaning the nation of Israel's sins generally, which included family treachery and strife at that period of their history. No-one could trust anyone else in his day of ministry. The Lord Jesus applied the sin to the treachery which would be shown by unbelieving members of a family towards those of them who did trust and obey Him as His disciples. Many believers have proved the truth of these words of Christ as they have made an open confession of Him, and have suffered as a result ostracism, rejection, and even martyrdom.

Its Outline

The seven short chapters of Micah may be divided into three sections, but there is some difference of opinion among commentators as to whether chapter 3 really belongs to the first or the second section. However, the majority view seems to be that it belongs to the second section. The deciding factor is the repetition of the opening words of the three major sermons, 'Hear ye', at chapter 1 verse 2, chapter 3 verse 1, and chapter 6 verse 1. There is a very pointed contrast between the end of chapter 3 and the first verses of chapter 4, which rather links the two chapters together than separates them into different sections of the book.

We present here three different, but quite similar, outlines of the book, which increase in detailed analysis. There is a recurring pattern of thought in the book. Each section begins with condemnations for particular sins, which are followed by announcements of coming judgement for those sins, but all these are concluded with predictive promises of ultimate restoration, salvation, and blessing for Israel through the Messiah, Christ. Even the first section covering chapters 1 to 2 concludes with two verses concerning the nation's deliverance through Christ.

Accordingly, we first present the shorter outline given by F.A. Tatford in his commentary on the Minor Prophets, which was republished recently by John Ritchie Ltd in Kilmarnock, as follows:

ANALYSIS OF MICAH

1. Judgment on Samaria and Judah (chapters 1 and 2).
    A) The Superscription   (1: 1).
    B) Judgment threatened   (1: 2-7).
    C) The prophet's lamentation   (1: 8-16).
    D) The causes of judgment   (2: 1-11).
    E) Restoration promised   (2: 12-13).

2. The Messianic salvation   (chapters 3 to 5).
    A) Sins of the nation's leaders   (3: 1-12).
    B) Vision of restoration   (4: 1-5: 1).
    C) The Messianic deliverance   (5: 2-15).

3. Jehovah's controversy   (chapters 6 and 7).
    A) The Divine case   (6: 1-16).
    B) Confession and repentance   (7: 1-14).
    C) The Divine promise   (7: 15-17).
    D) Final doxology   (7: 18-20).

Introduction to Micah's Prophecy

Dr Tatford notes that the three discourses probably represent a far larger number of oral messages. Each discourse begins with a call to hear, and concludes with a promise. He further notes that there is a two-fold strand in Micah's messages: denunciation on the one side and comfort on the other. Sin is first exposed and then the promise of salvation and deliverance is presented. This pattern of thought is followed throughout the Scriptures and in the present-day gospel message.

Secondly, John MacArthur gives us a very similar outline in his *MacArthur Bible Commentary*, thus:

Outline of Micah

i.	Superscription	(1: 1)
ii.	God Gathers to Judge and Deliver	(1: 2-2: 13)
	A. Samaria and Judah Punished	(1: 2-16)
	B. Oppressors Judged	(2: 1-5)
	C. False Prophets Renounced	(2: 6-11)
	D. Promise of Deliverance	(2: 12-13)
iii.	God Judges Rulers and Comes to Deliver	(3: 1-5: 15)
	A. The Contemporary Leaders are Guilty	(3: 1-12)
	B. The Coming Leader will Deliver and Restore	(4: 1-5: 15)
iv.	God Brings Indictments and Ultimate Deliverance	(6: 1-7: 20)
	A. Messages of Reproof and Lament	(6: 1-7: 6)
	B. Messages of Confidence and Victory	(7: 7-20)

Thirdly, *The Bible Knowledge Commentary* gives us a more detailed outline than either of these, as follows:

OUTLINE OF MICAH

i.	First Message: Judgment Will Come	(chaps. 1-2)
	A. Introduction	(1: 1)
	B. Prediction of coming judgment	(1: 2-7)
	C. Lament over the people	(1: 8-16)
	1. Micah's lament	(1: 8-9)
	2. Micah's call for others to mourn	(1: 10-16)

D. Sins of Judah	(2: 1-11)
1. Sins of the people	(2: 1-5)
2. Sins of the false prophets	(2: 6-11)
E. Prediction of future regathering	(2: 12-13)
ii. Second Message: Blessing Will Follow Judgment	(chaps. 3-5)
A. Judgment on the nation's leaders	(chap. 3)
1. Judgment on the rulers	(3: 1-4)
2. Judgment on the false prophets	(3: 5-8)
3. Judgment on all the naive leaders	(3: 9-12)
B. Kingdom blessings for the nation	(chaps. 4-5)
1. Characteristics of the kingdom	(4: 1-8)
2. Events preceding the kingdom	(4: 9-5: 1)
3. The Ruler of the kingdom	(5: 2-15)
iii. Third Message: An Indictment of Sin and a Promise of Blessing	(chaps. 6-7)
A. An indictment by the Lord	(6: 1-5)
B. The response of Micah for the nation	(6: 6-8)
C. The Lord's judgment because of sin	(6: 9-16)
1. The sins	(6: 9-12)
2. The punishment	(6: 13-16)
D. Micah's pleading with the Lord	(chap. 7)
1. Micah's bemoaning of the nation's sins	(7: 1-6)
2. Micah's confidence in the Lord	(7: 7-13)
3. Micah's prayer that God would again shepherd His flock	(7: 14)
4. The Lord's promise to show miraculous things to His people	(7: 15-17)
5. Micah's affirmation that God is unique	(7: 18-20)

Its Main Searching Message for Today

Just as the LORD's people Israel in Micah's day needed to be confronted with their sins in all their horror and offence to God, and then warned of inevitable judgement coming soon upon them, so today we all need to be made acutely aware of our many sins against the majesty and holiness of God, and to be warned of

Introduction to Micah's Prophecy

coming judgement for them, both in the short-term and ultimately in the future. Our nations have all largely departed from the truth of God, and have rejected the Gospel of His Grace, turning to their own ideas of morality and righteousness, which are mostly condemned by God in His word. As a consequence, they are reaping a growing harvest of trouble and disorder, and yet they are obstinately refusing to acknowledge that the real cause of their difficulties is rebellion against the plain principles of Scripture. They seem to be prepared to listen to any other philosophy of life than the divine wisdom expounded in the Bible. Therefore, whenever the present-day preachers of the gospel address unbelievers, they need to stress the truths of sin and coming judgement as the necessary background for the message of God's grace and salvation in Christ. Otherwise, unsaved sinners will never see the need to repent and believe the Gospel. If there is no danger of going to hell and eternal punishment and torment, about which the Bible clearly warns us all, then our hearers will fail to see any need to listen to the message which we have been commissioned to preach. Yes, just as Micah first stressed the negative aspects of the LORD's message through him, predicting catastrophic events, such as the two exiles of Israel and Judah in Assyria and Babylon, as a punishment for His people's sins, so we today need to begin our gospel messages with parallel warnings concerning the universality of sin and coming judgement for it.

Secondly, just as Micah then presented the divine answer to this universal problem of sin and judgement in the Person of Christ, the Jews' Messiah, so we today need to explain to our hearers that, in every situation in our distressed lives, Christ and His salvation are the answer to our desperate need. Christ is referred to in several passages of Micah's Prophecy as God's remedy for His earthly people's sins and distress. At the end of chapter 2, after a long denunciation of Israel's sins, and therefore rather unexpectedly, Micah is inspired to predict the regathering of the remnant of Israel in the end times, and is led to introduce us to their Leader, who is here called the Breaker, that is, the One who enables them to break out of their captivity in their enemies' cities. In the last line of the chapter, He is identified as their King, and the LORD Himself, who is none other than the divine Christ.

Then, in chapters 4 and 5, Christ, again identified as the LORD, is predicted to be Israel's King reigning over them in Mount Zion, and even His birth-place, Bethlehem Ephratah, is predicted, as is also the fact that He will be 'the peace' when the latter-day Assyrian enemy invades Israel's land. All salvation, whether for Israel or for ourselves today, centres in Christ alone. Christ is the only and fully sufficient Answer to our deepest needs. Only, Micah is not inspired to reveal, as his contemporary prophet Isaiah was led to do, the means by which Christ secured our salvation on the cross of Calvary. He concentrates on the LORD's final salvation from the power of Israel's enemies, rather than from the penalty for their sins.

Thirdly, Micah does reveal the blessed effects of the final salvation of His wayward people Israel in the end times and Christ's Millennial Kingdom, when they will be completely restored both to their Promised Land and to great prosperity in a time of universal peace. He also predicts that the LORD, in the Person of Christ, will remove all idolatry from His people, so that He alone is worshipped. Micah does not appear to stress the necessity of repentance as much as other prophets do, but in chapter 6 verse 8, he clearly summarises God's moral requirements from mankind, which are the essential fruits of repentance and salvation. These are that we should all 'do justly', 'love mercy', and 'walk humbly' with Him, our God. The whole world will be a different, and much happier, place to live in when these characteristics mark all its inhabitants, as they will in the coming kingdom, because God's Holy Spirit will be permanently indwelling all believers on earth then. Again, Micah is not led to reveal this latter truth, as Jeremiah and Ezekiel were privileged to do. We need to read all Scripture to understand the whole truth of God. However, Christians today are indwelt by the Holy Spirit and are enabled by Him to fulfil the righteous requirements of the law of God in a way that Old Testament Israel was unable to do. We should therefore seek to live as God intended us to live, worshipping and pleasing Him alone, and loving our neighbours as ourselves. We have the Spirit of Christ within us, and should allow Him to live His perfect life of love and holiness through us day by day.

Introduction to Micah's Prophecy

These, then, are the three major strands of truth that we need to accept from Micah's prophecy as God's main searching message to us all, both unbelievers and present-day Christians: condemnation for sin, together with its inevitable judgement, both now and in eternity; the answer to our problems caused by sin in Christ alone; and the joyful and peaceful fruit of a changed life resulting from our restoration to God at conversion or after a period of backsliding from Him. Finally, we discover from the last section of Micah's Prophecy that there is no-one who can ever compare with God in His strong desire to pardon us despite all our sins against Him. His unconditional promises to us today as Christians, just as those made to His earthly people Israel's patriarchs several thousand years ago, are irrevocable and certain to be fulfilled quite literally at their right time in His prophetic calendar. Christ is our Deliverer from the coming wrath upon this rebellious world. He is coming again to receive us to Himself at the Resurrection and Rapture of the New Testament Church, when we shall reign with Him over His everlasting kingdom, after He has defeated all His and our foes. Hallelujah! What a Saviour!

Concise Commentary on Micah

Micah Chapter 1

1. *Micah's call by the LORD in a vision to prophesy to both the Israelite kingdoms centred on Samaria and Jerusalem, v. 1.*

This word, or revelation, from the LORD came to Micah the Morasthite in a vision at various times during the successive reigns of Jotham, Ahaz, and Hezekiah, kings of Judah. Micah ignored the kings of the Northern Kingdom of Israel, probably because they were not descended from the Davidic dynasty and were all evil. The kingdom of Israel was ended during Micah's ministry in 722 BC by the invasion of the Assyrian kings, who besieged Samaria for three years, and then carried its citizens captive into exile in their empire. Micah may have prophesied for about thirty-five or forty years, from about 740 BC until well into Hezekiah's reign, but may not have witnessed the siege of Jerusalem by Sennacherib in 701 BC. Although Micah here ignores the evil kings of the Northern Kingdom, it is explicitly stated that he prophesied concerning both parts of the Divided Monarchy, centred on their capital cities of Samaria and Jerusalem. Both kingdoms had become equally guilty of sin against their covenant-keeping LORD God, so the LORD led Micah to speak to all the people of Israel, and not just to his own kingdom of Judah.

2. *The LORD calls all peoples and creation to witness His declaration of imminent judgement upon both the kingdoms of Israel for their serious sins of idolatry and immorality against Him, vv. 2-7.*

The LORD speaks as Israel's sovereign, covenant-keeping Lord GOD from His holy temple in heaven, and is seen as an almighty giant coming down to tread on the high places of the earth, which had been misused in His people's idolatry. The mountains, valleys, and waterfalls will be disturbed under Him, causing earthquakes and volcanic activity. It is presented as a universal lawcourt scene, in which the LORD is the prosecuting counsel against both Samaria and Jerusalem for their transgressions of His holy law. The high places are specifically mentioned as the chief causes of His wrath. Jotham failed to prevent his citizens from worshipping false gods on them, according to 2 Kings chapter 15 verse 35, and Ahaz had encouraged their continued and increased use during his evil reign, while Hezekiah had attempted to reform this situation, but had not carried all his subjects with him. Idolatry had started in the Northern Kingdom of Israel under Jeroboam the son of Nebat with his calf-images, which had been intended to divert his people from worshipping the LORD at the true centre in Solomon's Temple in Jerusalem, where the LORD's Glory-cloud dwelt, but it had spread to the Southern Kingdom also by this time, and thus the whole of Israel had become virtually apostate. Judgement must follow swiftly, or the LORD's holy Name would be dishonoured in the world.

Therefore, in verses 6-7, the LORD declares that He will make Samaria, the corrupt capital of the Northern Kingdom, a heap of ruins, fit only to become a place for planting a vineyard. The fine buildings of stone in it would be poured down into the valley below its hill like waterfalls, and their foundations would be exposed. This happened during the capture of Samaria by the Assyrians in 722 BC. All the carved images in the city would be smashed to pieces, and all the love-gifts given to the false gods as part of their abominable ritual prostitution would be destroyed by fire. The wages of sin are terrible, and Samaria, the chief source of Israel's corruption, would receive her punishment in full measure.

3. Micah's lament over the sadness of his people's imminent fate, which was to reach even to the gate of Jerusalem, vv. 8-9.

Micah was a true patriot of his native country, despite his people's horrendous sins, and therefore was deeply distressed that they were about to suffer such disasters. As a sign of his mourning and grief he said that he would go barefoot and naked, and wail like jackals and owls, or perhaps ostriches. He realised that

Samaria's wound would be incurable, and also that the fate that overtook her would affect his own part of the Divided Kingdom, Judah, and reach to the very gate of Jerusalem. He anticipated the siege of Jerusalem in 701 BC by the proud Assyrian monarch, Sennacherib, who would boast that he had shut up Hezekiah in Jerusalem 'like a bird in a cage', according to his annals. Happily, the LORD would deliver Hezekiah from ultimate disaster then, because he truly trusted in Him, but later in 586 BC the Babylonian king, Nebuchadnezzar, would finally capture Jerusalem for the third time and carry away its citizens into the Babylonian exile. Hezekiah obtained a reprieve from the impending judgement, so Micah was correct in predicting that the danger would only reach to the gate of Jerusalem, but not then overwhelm the city. It is thought by some commentators that Micah may not have lived to see this first siege of Jerusalem in 701 BC, by contrast with his older contemporary prophet Isaiah, who recorded the LORD's miraculous defeat of Sennacherib's army by a plague inflicted by an angel in one night, and made this deliverance the centrepiece of his major prophetic book.

4. Micah anticipates the devastation that would befall the towns in southwest Judah when the Assyrians attacked them in 701 BC, and calls on their citizens to mourn for it, using Hebrew puns on the place-names to emphasise their distress, vv. 10-16.

Although Jerusalem would not fall to the Assyrians in 701 BC, most of the towns of Judah would fall to their army, before they reached the gate of Jerusalem. There would be great loss of life and possessions, as the Assyrians progressed through southwest Judah on their way from Egypt, which they would defeat first as Judah's ally, towards the capital, where Hezekiah would wait in trepidation concerning the outcome of the invasion. Micah singles out the names of many places which lay in the path of the Assyrian army, and graphically describes the serious effects of their invasion by playing on the sounds and meanings of their names in Hebrew. Several commentators and translators of these verses have made a good attempt to convey the effect of these puns. The places mentioned are all ones which would have been well-known to Micah, since he was a native of one of them, namely, Moresheth-gath in the low hill country southwest of Jerusalem near the country of the Philistines. His own hometown was to be overrun by these cruel Gentile warriors.

We will attempt to explain the puns. First, Micah exhorts his people not to tell the bad news in Gath, one of the five Philistine cities, whose name can bear the meaning 'Tell-town'. The Philistines would rejoice over Judah's misfortune as one of their chief enemies. 'Weep ye not at all' may mean that the towns of Judah should not let their enemies in Gath know by their tears that there is mourning in the land. Secondly, 'in the house of Aphrah roll thyself in the dust' is a pun on the place-name of the town called Beth Ophrah, which means 'house of dust'. Rolling oneself in dust was a sign of mourning. Thirdly, in verse 11, the town called Saphir, which means 'beautiful or pleasant', would become the opposite of its name, a town of nakedness and shame, as the inhabitants were made to go out into captivity. Similarly, the town of Zaanan, whose name sounds like the word for 'coming out', or 'marching', would not dare to go outside their city walls because of the threat of warfare there. They had failed to come to the aid of a neighbouring town called Beth-ezel, whose name means 'house of nearness or proximity'. That town was also in mourning. The NIV translation of the last part of this verse is, 'its protection is taken from you'. The townsfolk of Beth-ezel were unable to help anyone else. Then, in verse 12, Micah says, with sarcasm, that the inhabitants of a town called Maroth, whose name sounds like the Hebrew word for 'bitterness', would look in vain for good news, because disaster would descend upon them from the LORD's judgemental hand even to the gate of Jerusalem, as it did in 701 BC.

In verse 13, Micah turns to address the city of Lachish, which was one of the chief fortresses of Judah. Their inhabitants were told to take flight when the enemy approached. There is a pun on the word Lachish. This sounds like the Hebrew word *rekesh*, which means 'a team', here of horses, harnessed to assist the people's escape. Therefore, some translators have translated this part of the verse, 'Bind the chariot to the horse, O inhabitant of Horse-town'. Then Micah explains the great guilt of the people of Lachish, for which they are being judged. It is that the idolatrous sins of the Northern

Kingdom of Israel first infiltrated into the Southern Kingdom of Judah through the people of Lachish. They were thus especially responsible for the latter kingdom's decline and departure from the LORD. Therefore, verse 14 says that Micah's home town of Moresheth-gath would fall into the hands of the Assyrian enemy during their invasion, and become their inheritance. The name of this town means 'possession, or inheritance', so there is another pun on its name here. Then, the houses of Achzib, which means 'lie', would become a disappointment to the kings of Israel, that is, the Davidic dynasty in Judah, by failing to save the situation. False gods and idols are sometimes called 'lies' in the Old Testament, since they invariably disappoint their deluded worshippers.

Therefore, verse 15 says that the LORD would bring an heir, or conqueror, to the inhabitants of Mareshah, which means 'inheritance'. There is a pun here on the words *hayyoresh* and *mareshah*. The heir, or conqueror, would be Sennacherib. The last part of the verse should probably be translated thus, 'the glory of Israel will enter Adullam' (NASB). The nobles of Judah would be compelled to take refuge in the cave of Adullam, as David and his mighty men had once done, when escaping from Saul.

The sarcasm of these puns must have been very biting and frightening for the people of Judah to listen to, threatening them with imminent disaster, and we trust that it may have led some of them to repent of their sins against their LORD God, whose covenant they had so seriously broken.

Finally, in verse 16, Micah calls on his people to mourn like a mother who has been bereft of her children, making themselves bald for their precious lost children, like an eagle, for they would go into captivity. Here Micah anticipates not just the invasion of Judah by the Assyrians in 701 BC, but looks forward to the later Babylonian exiles of citizens of Judah by Nebuchadnezzar from 605 to 586 BC. His people's sins would reap a terrible harvest.

Micah Chapter 2

1. The LORD through Micah pronounces a woe of judgement upon His people for their many sins against His covenant, especially those of the rich and influential landowners for oppressing the poor, vv. 1-5.

Having warned God's people in chapter 1 of the judgement coming to them, Micah now pronounces a woe on them for particular sins of oppression of the poor, of which the rich landowners were especially guilty. Sadly, the acquisition of wealth and material prosperity often leads men to commit sins of social injustice; such is the utter selfishness of the human heart. These unscrupulous men lay in bed at night planning their wicked schemes, and in the morning they put them into practice, because they had the ability and opportunity to do so. They deprived people of their inherited property, blatantly ignoring the commandments in the Mosaic Law concerning the perpetual ownership by each Jewish citizen of the land which had originally been given to them by lot. According to Leviticus chapter 25 verse 13, even if a man had been compelled to sell his land to a creditor because of poverty, that property should revert to him as the original owner in the year of Jubilee. This provision in the Law was intended to prevent anyone becoming either very poor, or very rich; it was good social justice. In any case, the whole of the Promised Land belonged first and foremost to the LORD their God, and no-one could treat it as his sole possession; all Israelites were simply the LORD's tenants. However, during the eighth century BC, in both parts of the Israelite kingdom, material success and increasing affluence had encouraged the wealthy citizens to ignore these wise provisions of their divinely given Law with disastrous results for the poorer citizens.

Therefore, in verses 3 to 5, the LORD announces to these

lawbreakers their appointed punishment. He says that He also is devising a plan: a disaster against them from which they would be unable to escape. They would not be able to continue in their arrogant attitude, because they would be facing a very calamitous time, which would humiliate them. In that day when the calamity occurred, which would be a time when the LORD intervened in their lives in judgement, a mourner amongst them would make a proverbial utterance against them, and lament bitterly, saying that, 'We have been utterly destroyed. The LORD has exchanged the inheritance of my people. See, how He has removed it from me! He has apportioned our fields to the apostate Gentiles!' This anticipated the imminent invasions by the Assyrians and the later Babylonians. Therefore, the LORD said, these men would have no-one to stretch out a surveyor's measuring-line according to the lot cast in the congregation of the LORD's people. In other words, they would lose all their inheritance in the invasions.

2. The LORD through Micah protests against those who tell Him not to prophesy concerning coming disaster, saying that, otherwise, the nation would suffer reproach and shame for their many sins, some of which He then explains, and He orders His corrupt people to go into captivity, since they would rather be preached to by false and irresponsible prophets than His own true prophets, vv. 6-11.

The covetous landowners refused to listen to the words of the LORD's true prophets warning them of coming disaster, and told them not to prophesy at all. The LORD replied that, unless they did speak out, the whole nation would suffer and become a reproach to their enemies. Micah and his true fellow-prophets could not prophesy blessing at that time, because the people's ways were not right. It was not that the Spirit of the LORD was unwilling or unable to speak of blessing, but rather that the nation's sins must first be corrected, before He could do so. He now explains some of their grievous social sins of injustice. They were robbing the poor and helpless and evicting defenceless widows from their pleasant houses, even taking away from their orphaned children the food, clothing, and shelter which had been given to them as a result of God's blessing on them, and which thus reflected God's glory towards them.

For these serious sins the LORD through Micah ordered these wicked landowners to get up and go out into captivity, because His Promised Land had become defiled by their wickedness. It was no longer their land of godly rest, as had been intended. They faced destruction in it and exile from it. The terms of the Palestinian Covenant in Deuteronomy chapters 28-30 had made Israel's continued occupation of the land dependent upon their obedience to the Mosaic Law, which they had repeatedly and unrepentantly broken. Sarcastically, the LORD said that, if a false prophet who prophesied irresponsibly about wine and strong drink, were to offer to minister to His people, he would be accepted by them rather than His true prophets. Thus the threat of invasion and exile faced them in the near future.

However, at this low point in the prophecy, the LORD inspires Micah to change his tone and predict ultimate future blessing for His wayward people, as He does so often throughout the prophetic Scriptures. Israel's LORD God is the God of recovery, who delights in blessing, not in judgement, and does not willingly afflict His people without good cause.

3. The LORD promises to regather the whole remnant of Israel, and to bring them out of captivity with their divine Shepherd/King at their head, vv. 12-13.

Here the LORD encourages the faithful remnant of true believers among His people with a glimpse of coming hope and glory by promising that He will regather all the remnant of Israel in a yet future day of restoration. The whole nation will be reunited at the time of this restoration. He will reassemble them like the sheep of Bozrah, which was a famous sheep-rearing region in Edom. The remnant returning to their Promised Land will become such a large multitude that their sound will resemble thousands of sheep bleating contentedly under the tender care of their divine Shepherd. This regathering and return from exile looks forward, beyond the partial return from Babylon in the time of Zerubbabel, Ezra, and Nehemiah in the sixth and fifth centuries BC, to the end times and the beginning of Christ's Millennial Kingdom. Then Christ will be personally present and lead the return and restoration Himself, having just been manifested from heaven at

His glorious second coming. The present continuing return of the Jews from all parts of the world to Israel is the beginning of the fulfilment of this prophecy, but this process, guided by the LORD Himself, is as yet far from complete, and will only finish after the sad events of the Tribulation have taken place.

However, verse 13 is a Messianic prophecy of the role which Christ will play in this regathering. He will be the One called the Breaker, the leading Shepherd, who breaks through all the obstacles that are hindering them from fully realising this prophecy at present. Now they are still scattered all over the world in various different countries, but, remarkably, have never been fully absorbed into the cultures and ways of any of them; they remain quite distinct from their immediate environments. They are waiting for their King, the Lord Jesus Christ, to appear to lead them to victory over their enemies and into His eternal kingdom. He is here identified with the LORD Himself, eternally divine and one with the Godhead. This is one Scripture that states that the Messiah of Israel is none other than God Himself, which fact many devout orthodox Jews today still doubt. Believing Jews do accept this truth, however, wholeheartedly.

Chapter 2 thus ends on a high and joyful note amid the gloom both of its preceding verses and of the chapter which follows. This alternating pattern of condemnation for sin with consequent pronouncements of coming judgement set side by side with glorious passages of future hope, restoration, and blessing for Israel is quite typical of most of the Old Testament prophetic books. Both ministries are always necessary when the LORD is dealing with a sinful people who are also in an unconditional covenant relationship with Him. There is a very similar pointed juxtaposition of judgement and glory at the end of chapter 3, to which we now turn.

Chapters 1 and 2 form the first major section of Micah's book, while chapters 3-5 form the second section.

Micah Chapter 3

1. The LORD through Micah summons Israel's leaders to hear Him pronounce judgement upon them for their violent oppression of His people, vv. 1-4.

The pervasive corruption that had affected the whole of Israel's Divided Kingdoms during the eighth century BC was particularly evident amongst the nation's leaders, both princes and ruling authorities. A nation often follows the lead of its leaders, whether for good or ill, and in Israel's case this was definitely for ill. Faithful believers and their spokesmen, the true prophets, usually find that they are a tiny minority swimming strenuously against the general tide of evil.

Here, the LORD through Micah is addressing the leaders of both kingdoms, since He identifies them as leaders of Jacob and Israel. All were equally guilty. He remonstrates with them that they, of all people, should know what true justice is, but evidently their consciences were seared with a hot iron. They hated what was good, and loved what was evil, calling good evil and evil good, as many do today in our current permissive society. His fellow-prophet Isaiah noted the same sad situation in about this same period of Israel's history, according to Isaiah chapter 5 verse 20. They had no conscience about fleecing their innocent and vulnerable citizens by all means in their power. They did not care for their charges at all, nor value them, but butchered and devoured them, so that they could take advantage of what little they had for their own selfish and wicked ends.

Therefore, the LORD declared that He would repay them in kind. When these leaders cried to Him for help in the day of calamity that was imminent, He would refuse to listen to them or to help them in any way, hiding His face from their desperate plight, since it had been brought on by their evil deeds. They would reap exactly what they had sown, as all men do, for good or ill. Just as they had ignored the cries of their victims of cruelty and injustice, so He would ignore them in their own hour of need.

Even Christians who are in any position of power and influence in their local churches need to be reminded that they should act with strict justice and compassion towards their fellow-saints in those churches, fully recognising their particular weaknesses and problems, being always kind, even if sometimes firm, in their relationships with them all. In 3 John the aged apostle John, who had once been known as 'a son of thunder', but who later became known as the apostle of love, wrote very severely concerning a certain dominant member of a local church called Diotrephes, who had arrogated too much power to himself and even wished to exclude the apostle himself from the church he controlled. No, Christians should be very careful and conscientious when they exercise any measure of authority and responsibility, whether in the local church, at work, or in their own household. We all have a Master in heaven who is watching us with a view to reviewing our service in every sphere of life and witness. Live in the light of the Judgement Seat of Christ!

2. The LORD further pronounces judgement upon the false prophets of Israel, who were prophesying peace simply to please the people and for money, and says that they would be afflicted with spiritual darkness and become ashamed to speak, by vivid contrast with Micah, His true prophet, who was filled with the Spirit, spoke justice with spiritual power, and preached to all Israel concerning their sin, vv. 5-8.

Now the LORD through Micah turned to condemn the false prophets in Israel, who were leading His people astray. When they had something to bite with their teeth, that is, as long as they were supplied with their daily food, they prophesied that peace and prosperity would come, and not disaster or invasion. Thus they tickled the ears of their listeners in order to earn their living from them; they had no concern to find out or preach the true word of the LORD. In fact, they became hostile towards those who failed to give them anything to eat.

Therefore, the LORD declared that these false prophets would be overcome with spiritual darkness; they would receive no vision from Himself, nor from their idolatrous divination. They would experience a total spiritual sunset, so that they would have no message at all to preach. These blind spiritual leaders of the people would become so ashamed of themselves that they would not dare to open their mouths nor to boast of their false profession to be prophets, but would cover their lips like unclean lepers, since they had received no answer from God, and would remain silent.

Micah, on the other hand, now asserted that he was full of the Spirit of the LORD, and endued with power to speak of justice and with true moral courage as he declared to all Israel their serious transgressions of the Law of God and their failures as His people. Assurance of the truth gives holy boldness to speak out against evil with the help of the Spirit of God. Micah was not a mercenary religionist like the false prophets, but sent from the LORD Himself with an urgent message from his LORD God to the people he loved. What are our true motives in ministry? Is it self-gratification or Christ's glory?

3. *Micah now predicted the judgement of the nation's leaders who were perverting all justice, acting with callous cruelty, and doing everything for monetary gain, yet still imagined that the LORD was among them, so that no calamity could ever befall them; the judgement for their sins was that Jerusalem would become a heap of ruins and Solomon's Temple would be destroyed, vv. 9-12.*

These final verses of the chapter contain another summons by the LORD through Micah to the nation's corrupt leaders to listen to His word and to understand the nature of the judgement that was imminent. We know from Jeremiah chapter 26 verses 18-19 that Micah made this prediction of judgement during the reign of the good king Hezekiah, and that he was not accused of treason for doing so, unlike Jeremiah later in the reign of the evil king Jehoiakim. We note in this present passage that, while the leaders of the nation were severely censured for their wickedness, the reigning king Hezekiah was not criticised. Evidently, although he himself was righteous, he was unable to fully control his covetous and cruel subordinate officials, despite the fact that he did effect quite thorough reforms during his reign. At least, Hezekiah was able to protect Micah's life, so that the latter probably died a natural death in peace during his reign.

Micah here summarises his charges against Israel's leaders by saying that they hated all justice and perverted all that was right and fair. He concentrates his righteous wrath on the leaders of Zion and Jerusalem, probably because, by the time that he prophesied this, the Northern Kingdom of Israel had already been conquered by the Assyrians in 722 BC and carried away into exile. Judah had learned nothing from their sister-kingdom's fate, and their leaders had continued to build up their capital city at the cost of extortion, judicial murder, and the misery of the poor. Wealth gained at the cost of destroying the rightful owners of property was used to further the selfish interests of the leaders. All the nation's officials wanted to be paid for their services, before they were willing to do anything. The judges required bribes, the priests only agreed to teach the people if they received payment, while the false prophets wanted money for their nefarious art of divination, which was itself idolatrous and forbidden. Yet, hypocritically, these false prophets professed to be relying on the LORD, and imagined vainly that He was still present among them, approving of them, and therefore that no calamity could ever befall the nation, ignoring the recent terrible fate of neighbouring Samaria and the Northern Kingdom of Israel. How blind, foolish, and self-deceived, hypocrites are! May the LORD preserve us from ever becoming like them!

Therefore, in verse 12, Micah predicts the coming judgement in no uncertain terms. Far from being spared the same fate as Samaria, the hill of Zion, once the city of David, and the whole of Jerusalem, the so-called City of Peace, would be completely destroyed, ploughed up like a field, and become just a heap of rubble. Even the far-famed Temple of Solomon, until then the dwelling-place of the LORD's Glory-cloud, would be destroyed and become like the bare hills in the forest. This prediction was fulfilled in 586 BC, when the Babylonian monarch, Nebuchadnezzar, who was the

LORD's servant in his invasion of Judah, razed the city and temple to the ground and carried all the remaining citizens of Judah into exile in Babylon for a full seventy years. Sin pays deadly wages in every sphere of life, and God is no respecter of persons in His righteous judgement. Let us fear to offend Him and thus incur His deserved wrath like ancient Israel!

Micah Chapter 4

1. In a pointedly contrasting prophecy concerning Jerusalem and the temple mount, the LORD reassures His people Israel that in the last days, the Millennial Reign of Christ, the temple will be rebuilt, its mountain elevated above the surrounding hills, and that all the Gentile nations will come to it to learn there the ways of the LORD, with the result that there will be universal peace and tranquillity in the world, vv. 1-5.

The chapter division here tends to obscure the clearly intended contrast between the end of chapter 3 and the beginning of chapter 4. Here the LORD through Micah suddenly predicts the ultimate glory and peace of Jerusalem in the yet future Millennial Kingdom of Christ, by vivid contrast with its imminent destruction at the time of the Babylonian captivity by Nebuchadnezzar in 586 BC. Isaiah also saw in a vision the same vivid contrast in chapter 2 of his own prophecy, where verses 2-4 are almost identical with verses 1-3 in this chapter of Micah. However, the next few verses in Micah's prophecy here are not found in Isaiah chapter 2, and Isaiah goes on to speak, not concerning the now fulfilled destruction of Jerusalem and Solomon's Temple, as is found in Micah chapter 3 verse 12, but concerning the yet future Day of the LORD, the judgements of the Tribulation. We have already referred to these partly-parallel passages in the Introduction, and have stated that it is difficult, if not impossible, to decide which prophet was quoting the other, or whether both of them were quoting a common source independently of one another. Their ministries certainly overlapped; Micah was marginally the younger of the two of them, but may well have died before Isaiah.

However that may be, we have here in chapter 4 a glimpse of the coming glory of Christ's kingdom based upon Jerusalem. After all the devastation of the preceding judgements spanning many centuries of Israel's sad history, from the time of the Babylonian invasion in 586 BC through the destruction of the city in AD 70 by Titus to the very worst time of its people's history during the future Tribulation, Micah is inspired to predict the complete restoration of both the city and the temple in the latter days, when Christ returns to this world to reign universally from Jerusalem to the ends of the earth. God will always have the last word in this world! As Zechariah chapter 14 indicates, Jerusalem will then be supernaturally elevated above its present altitude to a position of great prominence, and the surrounding land will become a level plain, so that both the city and its temple will be clearly seen from all directions, being the centre of the earth and the world's capital. Ezekiel chapters 40-48 predict the construction and worship of the new Millennial Temple, which Christ will build with the help of the world's surviving citizens, believing Jews and Gentiles. The LORD will be there; His Glory-cloud will return to dwell there permanently. Many peoples and nations who have believed on Christ during the preceding terrible years of the Tribulation will flow willingly and spontaneously up to it and ask to be taught the ways of the LORD and His word.

The LORD, in the Person of Christ, will arbitrate between many peoples, and initially, probably in the judgements which must precede the beginning of the Millennial Kingdom, rebuke strong nations who have earlier opposed Him. All offensive weapons will be converted into useful agricultural implements, and there will be universal peace among the nations, so that no-one will learn how to conduct war any more. Rather, all nations will live in peace and enjoy complete security and prosperity, every one sitting unmolested under his and her own vine and fig trees. No-one will try to terrify them. If this seems unlikely or impossible of fulfilment, then just consider that the One who has spoken this prophecy is none other than the omnipotent LORD of hosts Himself, the Commander of all armies in heaven and earth, and thus it is certain to happen one day, and perhaps quite soon.

Verse 5 needs to be read in a more recent translation to understand its probable meaning clearly. The AV/KJV translation suggests that the prophet is predicting that in the coming Millennial Kingdom every nation will worship the true God under the name of its own god, that is, its false idolatrous god. Rather, Micah is declaring that, although the heathen Gentile peoples *now* worship their own particular false gods, Israel, in the coming time of peace and glory just described, will be in a state of spiritual blessing and prosperity, because they will be worshipping the eternal God and living in His power and strength alone. They will at last be cured of the grievous sin of idolatry.

2. The LORD further promises that, 'in that day', the beginning of Christ's Millennial Kingdom, He will regather all Israel, including the infirm and the afflicted, and transform them into a strong nation for Him to rule over in a restored Jerusalem, vv. 6-8.

Again, as at the end of chapter 2, the LORD promises to regather all His scattered people Israel, whatever their sad condition, whether lame, outcast, or suffering the effects of His chastisement, and forge them into a true believing remnant and a strong nation during Christ the LORD's Millennial Reign, and beyond that time into eternity forever. The nation would be completely restored in mount Zion. Then, in verse 8, the LORD addresses Jerusalem, in view of her prominence and elevation during the Kingdom Age, as the lofty tower of the flock, from which Christ, His Shepherd/King, would guard His flock of true believers like a stronghold. Jerusalem's former dominion over the surrounding nations would be recovered for her, and she would enjoy all the political and religious prestige that she lost after David's and Solomon's time, when Rehoboam caused the division of the Israelite kingdom in 931 BC. Ezekiel chapter 37 also anticipates the reunification of the Divided Monarchy at the beginning of the Millennial Kingdom.

3. Returning to the time of Micah, the LORD likens the city of Jerusalem to a woman writhing in childbirth, and states that she will go into captivity in Babylon, but then promises that she will be redeemed from there out of the power of her enemies, vv. 9-10.

The next two short sections return initially to the plight of Jerusalem in the time of Micah and a little later, but also seem to anticipate both the return from exile in Babylon and the yet future final campaign of Armageddon against Jerusalem at the end of the

Tribulation. In verses 9-10, the prophet asks his people based in Jerusalem why they are crying out in pain like a woman suffering birth pangs. Did they really have no king or counsellor to protect and guide them? The implication is that His people had rejected the LORD as their Ruler and Counsellor, and thus had fallen into trouble. The figure of childbirth suggests that the LORD is implying that, although Israel's labour pains would eventually lead to better and happier times ahead, His people had to endure very distressing times before they were delivered from all their difficulties and could enjoy the blessings that He had just been predicting for them.

It is a remarkable evidence of Micah's divine inspiration that he spoke here not of the immediate threat from the Assyrians, as he had earlier in his book, but looked quite beyond this to the future Babylonian invasions of 605 to 586 BC, and predicted the exile of Judah to Babylon then. The LORD also inspired him to reassure His people that He would redeem them from there back to their own land out of the clutches of their enemies. The books of Ezra and Nehemiah record the partial return of the Jews from Babylon in the sixth and fifth centuries BC. God fulfilled His word then.

However, while the immediate interpretation of these verses refers primarily to the Old Testament Babylonian exile, the following few verses probably foreshadow a greater travail in the days of the yet future Tribulation, out of which Israel will again be saved to enter the future kingdom of Christ.

4. The LORD says to Jerusalem that, although many nations were gathering to gloat over her destruction, they failed to realise that He had gathered them, in order that Israel might defeat them all in the end times, vv. 11-13.

These few verses tend to confirm the view that a yet future scene is in mind here, besides the more immediate prediction of the Assyrian and Babylonian threats of invasion. Several times throughout history many nations have gathered around Jerusalem with the intention of destroying her once and for all, but she has always emerged from these experiences to face the future again.

Revelation chapter 16 reveals that this will happen again towards the end of the Great Tribulation, but that, as these verses in Micah also state, the LORD will be orchestrating the whole grim scene during the campaign of Armageddon in order to bring His judgement on the enemies of Israel. Also, a few other Scriptures in Isaiah and Zechariah confirm this, and reveal that the LORD will empower and use His restored people Israel to defeat His and their enemies when Christ returns in glory to this sad world again to take up His great power and reign. The LORD will use Israel to devote their enemies' unjust gain and wealth to Christ as the sovereign Lord of all the earth. What a day of righting all wrongs that will be! No, as Isaiah said in chapter 54 verse 17 of his prophecy, no weapon formed against His people Israel will ever ultimately prosper, although God will use their enemies to chastise them severely for their former apostasy and unbelief. God's people Israel are as indestructible as He is Himself, see also Jeremiah chapter 33 verses 23-26! Praise His Name, for this reassures us who believe today that our salvation is also perfectly secure despite all our own failings!

Micah Chapter 5

1. The LORD exhorts Jerusalem to muster her military forces, because her enemies have besieged her, and they will even insult the judge of Israel by striking him on the cheek, v. 1.

In the Hebrew Bible, this verse is the last verse of chapter 4, which fact alters all the verse numbers in the following chapter 5 in the original Hebrew editions of the Old Testament. Verse 1 in our English Bibles has proved somewhat difficult to interpret with complete certainty. However, the first part of the verse, 'Now muster yourselves in troops, daughter of troops' (NASB), probably returns to the thought in verses 9 and 10 of chapter 4, which anticipate the siege of Jerusalem by the Babylonians. Jerusalem is addressed as the 'daughter of troops', both because she is full of soldiers to defend the city, and because she is going to be besieged by the invading Babylonians. The LORD exhorts her to marshal all her troops for the defence of the city. He says that the invaders will insult the ruler of Israel by striking him on the cheek. When the Babylonians captured Jerusalem and her king, Zedekiah, in 586 BC, they treated him very despicably and even put out his eyes, see 2 Kings 25. Some commentators have thought, in view of the Messianic nature of verse 2, that 'the judge of Israel' referred to here is the Lord Jesus Christ, who was certainly humiliated during His mock trial and death in a similar way. However, the primary reference in this verse is probably to the Old Testament king Zedekiah, because Christ was not struck in any siege, nor struck with a rod, nor by a foreign enemy, but by His own people. When king Zedekiah was struck and mistreated, Israel was suffering the reproach of their sins, which had caused the Babylonian exile to take place. In these immediate chapters, the LORD through Micah is moving backwards and forwards in time. At the end of chapter 4, He had been predicting the distant future, whereas here the word 'Now' probably indicates that He is returning to the nearer future from Micah's point of view.

2. By contrast with Zedekiah, the eternal Christ Himself, the true future Ruler of Israel, although born in obscurity in Bethlehem Ephratah, will arise to shepherd Israel, after they have suffered greatly, and, when their latter-day Assyrian enemy invades their country, will through His greatness ensure His people's peace by delivering them, vv 2-6.

In verse 2, the first word 'But' indicates a complete contrast with the thoughts of verse 1, where the failing king Zedekiah was predicted to be humiliated and degraded by Israel's enemies. Verse 2 introduces us to the true future Ruler of Israel, who would have very humble circumstances for His birth, but rise to greatness in the nation in the end times. This verse predicts the exact place where the Lord Jesus was to be born, as the Jewish religious rulers recognised at the time of His birth, according to Matthew chapter 2, but failed to acknowledge Him, unlike the wise men from the east. The small town of Bethlehem Ephratah in Judah is here distinguished from the other town called Bethlehem in the region of Galilee, which was allocated to the tribe of Zebulun, according to Joshua chapter 19 verse 15. Bethlehem means 'house of bread', while Ephratah means 'fruitful', referring to the fertility of the region. Thus it was very appropriate that the true benevolent Ruler of Israel should originate historically from such a place. However, Christ's origin was not really only from Bethlehem, but from eternity, since He had always been the Son of the Father and in His bosom. At His birth He came forth into time to become Israel's King with a divine commission to fulfil all His Father's will for that nation.

Verse 3, however, states that, because of what was predicted in verse 2, Christ's birth in the lowly town of Bethlehem, rather than the capital Jerusalem, could only mean that the dynasty of David had fallen on evil days, and that Israel had been given up into the power of their enemies. Although Israel's Messiah had already been born, the nation of Israel failed to recognise Him, and actually crucified Him as if He were an impostor. Therefore, the LORD has, in discipline, given them up to suffer great travail,

Concise Commentary on Micah chapter 5

until they are ready to accept Him in the end times. During the coming Tribulation they will suffer unparalleled pain, until Christ returns in glory to deliver them during the campaign of Armageddon, when they will at last recognise who their true Saviour is, the pierced Man of Calvary, see Zechariah chapter 12. Then the faithful remnant of Israel will welcome Him, and the scattered Jews from all countries of the world will return to their brethren in the Promised Land of Israel at the beginning of Christ's Millennial Kingdom. After that reunion with His chosen earthly people, Christ will shepherd them as His flock and ensure their security from all their enemies by His divine strength. His divine majesty and greatness will be recognised throughout the world He made, and He will bring peace to the troubled nation of Israel as their long-awaited Prince of Peace.

In the second half of verse 5, Micah is inspired to predict that Christ will deliver Israel in the future, when their latter-day Assyrian enemy invades their country, according to Daniel chapter 11 verses 40-45. Other Scriptures in the earlier chapters of Isaiah may also predict this future invasion by 'the Assyrian'. When the future Assyrian enemy tramples on Israel's citadels, and threatens to overwhelm them, Christ will protect them by raising up against them 'seven shepherds and eight principal men'. Seven is the number of perfection, or completeness, while eight suggests something more than is necessary, an abundance of help. These men will be chosen princes of the Chief Shepherd of Israel, specially empowered to defend His people, perhaps the heroes mentioned in Zechariah chapter 12 as defending Jerusalem. However, they will not only defend Israel, but also carry the battle into their enemies' country, the land of Assyria, where Nimrod, the first rebel hunter against the LORD, built the first empire from the city of Babel, which is the origin of Babylon. Christ will extend His rule to that country also, and thus completely and finally deliver Israel from their Assyrian enemy, when he foolishly dares to trample on their territory.

3. During Christ's Millennial Kingdom the restored faithful remnant of Israel will act like refreshing dew and seasonal showers upon all the surrounding nations of the world, a blessing

to all of them, and they will be empowered to act like lions to destroy all their enemies, vv. 7-9.

The apostle Peter in Acts chapter 3 verse 19 spoke of these 'times of refreshing from the presence of the LORD', meaning the blessings which will be bestowed upon the world when Christ returns in glory to reign in His Millennial Kingdom. When He is accepted, and when Israel is in their rightful place as the chief nation on earth, they will act like refreshing dew and needful showers on the dry ground of this sinful world after all its previous Tribulation judgements and wars, and all its sinful history. They will bring untold blessing to everyone in the kingdom. However, where enemies of the LORD and of Israel have dared to raise their heads in rebellion, they will be empowered to act like lions to destroy them. Israel's enemies will all be destroyed by the beginning of Christ's rule.

4. Now the LORD says that, in that day of His Millennial Kingdom, He will destroy all the military weapons and resources upon which Israel had previously been relying, rather than upon Himself, and also destroy all their idolatrous images and occult equipment to which they had resorted instead of to Him, and execute His wrath upon the disobedient Gentile nations, vv. 10-15.

Now the LORD declared that, in that coming millennial day, probably right at its commencement, He will take every precaution to remove from Israel all the things upon which they had previously been relying for defence and guidance rather than trusting in Him. These included their military equipment in the form of horses and chariots, which they had been forbidden to multiply from the time of Moses, and all their military fortresses. Further, He would destroy all their witchcrafts and fortune-tellers, which they had used to guide them instead of seeking His guidance; also their carved idolatrous images, sacred pillars, and Asherah poles, which they had used to worship the work of their own hands. The Mosaic Law forbade evil forms of worship and gaining guidance in life from the occult. Finally, the LORD asserted that He would take vengeance on all the disobedient Gentile nations who had refused to accept His rule before. How different the whole world will be then, when our Lord Jesus

Christ, who is also Israel's Messiah, reigns for a full thousand years from Jerusalem without a rival! It will very largely be a reign of peace, prosperity and joy. Maranatha! Hasten the day of His glory!

Micah Chapter 6

1. Returning now to Micah's own times, the LORD summons all creation to witness His serious complaint against His people Israel, asking them why they had become weary of following Him in spite of all that He had done to help them, vv. 1-5.

Chapters 6 and 7 form the third and final section of Micah's prophecy, and verse 1 begins in the same way as chapters 1 and 3 with a summons by the LORD to hear Him. Chapter 6 takes the form of a courtroom scene, in which the LORD is the prosecutor and Israel is the defendant, while the witnesses and jury are all creation everywhere, here specifically the mountains and hills. Other prophets also call on inanimate nature to witness the LORD's complaint, or controversy, against Israel, in order to emphasise the enormity of human sin; see Deuteronomy 32 verse 1; Isaiah 1 verse 2; Jeremiah 2 verses 12-13. It is amazing to consider that the sovereign LORD of the universe should condescend to reason with His creatures at all, rather than simply judge them summarily.

Twice, in verses 3 and 5, the LORD addresses Israel kindly as 'O My people', and remonstrates with them for their base ingratitude towards Him after all He has done for them throughout their history. He asks them how He has offended them, or wearied them with His gracious ways. After all, He had brought them up out of their hard slavery in Egypt, and redeemed them at great cost by the blood of the Passover Lamb and by power at the Red Sea. He had given them good leaders in Moses, Aaron, and Miriam, who were, respectively, the law-giver, the high priest, and the song-leader at the Red Sea. Also, later on, He had delivered them from the wicked schemes devised by Balak, king of Moab, and by Balaam, the son of Beor, an apostate false prophet. He asked them to remember all that happened on the way from Shittim to Gilgal: the seduction of some of the nation by the Moabite women; their deliverance through the javelin of Phinehas; then the miraculous crossing of the flooded River Jordan into the Promised Land. He had defended and protected them all through their wilderness journey. Did they not recognise and acknowledge His absolute righteousness in all His dealings with them? Surely He was not to blame, but they themselves were, because of their constant waywardness.

2. Micah, replying on behalf of the people, asks rhetorically how they should approach the LORD acceptably, and gives the answer that they should not just come with costly ritual sacrifices, but live a righteous, merciful, and humble life with the LORD their God, vv. 6-8.

These few verses are central to the message that Micah gave to Israel from the LORD concerning the way in which they could please Him. The nation stood convicted of their guilt, and Micah asks, on their behalf, how they can remedy the sad situation. What exactly did the LORD require from them? After all, He is so great and holy, and we are all so weak and sinful. Does He require thousands of expensive burnt offerings of the best young calves and rams to prove our devotion to Him? Or myriads of rivers of olive oil? Even perhaps the human sacrifice of our first-born sons, supposedly to atone for the sin of our souls?

How often the LORD's chosen earthly people had attempted to please their God with such ritual sacrifices, but He had told them that He did not, first and foremost, require anything like this at all! Rather, they should have known from their own Law of Moses that He required a whole life lived to His glory in ordinary practical ways. Here in verse 8, Micah, on the LORD's behalf, spells out the three basic moral and spiritual requirements for a godly life. From this we today should also learn how we can please our God. It is effectively a summary of the whole Law and Prophets in one verse. It applies to all men everywhere, not just to Israel. It is to behave righteously and fairly with everyone we know, to love to do merciful and kind things to others in need, and to live constantly in complete humility with our God. The world will be a completely different place when all men are enabled by the Spirit of God to live like this! How do we today measure up to these basic requirements in our lives? Micah had been obliged to condemn his contemporaries for their unjust, unkind, and arrogant manner of life in the eighth century BC, and we see these same sins prevalent in our own day and society. May the LORD enable us, by His grace and through His indwelling Holy Spirit, to fulfil these moral and spiritual requirements in large measure in our own generation, which is just as needy, as well as sinful, as Micah's generation!

3. Micah introduces the LORD's voice again calling to the city of Jerusalem to listen to His corrective rod in view of their continued sins of injustice, oppression, and deceit, vv. 9-12.

However, far from being characterised by these latter virtues just outlined to them by the LORD's prophet Micah, Israel was marked by some of the most glaring sins. Therefore, the LORD must punish the citizens of Jerusalem, which was undoubtedly the centre of all such wrong practices. The LORD was through Micah calling to His people to listen to His corrective judgement, which would soon fall upon them. The middle sentence of verse 9 has been translated in various ways by different translators, as follows: 'the man of wisdom shall see Thy name', that is, shall regard God in His revelations of Himself; or, 'the man of wisdom shall fear Thy name', that is, shall reverence the LORD; or, 'wisdom has Thy name in its eye', that is, has God's glory in view; or again, 'there is deliverance for those who fear Thy name'. Feinberg states that only slight changes in the original Hebrew text are required to obtain these different readings. He explains, 'the thought is that, when the voice of the LORD is lifted up to speak forth judgement, the man of wisdom sees the dealings of God that reveal His righteous character. Therefore, let all Israel similarly note the chastisement of God and who it is that has brought it about'. When the nation would begin to accept the justice and righteousness of these chastisements by their LORD God, there could begin to be blessing again.

Verses 10-12 explain some of the sins which marked Israel at that time. First, the people were still accumulating wealth in their houses by wicked means. Secondly, they were dishonest in their business practices. They used a measure that was short of the full amount of an ephah, and thus cheated their customers. They were also using inaccurate scales and false weights to weigh out goods to their purchasers. Thirdly, the rich men among them were resorting to violent methods to oppress the poor and innocent. Finally, they were all marked by deceit in their speech to one another; no-one could trust anyone else's word. What a sad and decadent society!

4. The LORD through Micah now announced the imminent punishment for these sins, which they had committed because they had followed the laws of Omri and the wicked practices of Ahab, rather than the laws of the LORD, vv. 13-16.

The coming judgement for their sins would be dreadful, and make them ill, but it would only be a just retribution for their wickedness. Sin always pays deadly wages. The LORD, using various providential means, would strike them and make them destitute. They would derive no satisfaction from their hard work, and would suffer hunger and emptiness. All their attempts to remove their goods from the path of the invading enemy would be unavailing; the enemy would overtake them and kill them with the sword. This probably anticipates the future Babylonian invasions of Nebuchadnezzar in 605 to 586 BC, as well as the Assyrian conquest of the Northern Kingdom of Israel in 722 BC, unless the latter had already occurred at the time when Micah spoke or wrote these words. Their crops would fail, or they would not live to reap them. They would not have any oil with which to anoint their skin in the hot climate of their Promised Land, nor would they enjoy drinking sweet wine which they had prepared in the winepress.

Verse 16 explains what had led the LORD's people to behave as they had done for a considerable time. It was the influence of the unrighteous laws of Omri in the Northern Kingdom of Israel, which had infiltrated into the Southern Kingdom of Judah (through the city of Lachish, according to chapter 1 verse 13), and also the wicked practices of king Ahab in the ninth century BC, which were motivated by the corrupt and idolatrous worship of the Baals through his evil foreign wife Jezebel. Omri and Ahab were considered by the faithful in Israel to be the two worst kings of the Northern Kingdom of Israel, because they led their citizens into open apostasy from the LORD and His covenantal laws. During Ahab's reign, true prophets of the LORD were murdered, according to 1 Kings chapter 18 verses 3 to 4, and only a few faithful servants of God like Obadiah, Ahab's steward, who feared the LORD greatly, and the prophets Elijah and Elisha, stood up against the wicked king. The people of Judah in the eighth century BC were living according to just these principles and practices; they could therefore hardly expect anything other than judgement. In fact, the LORD warned them that He was going to make them an object of horror to everyone who saw them. The latter would hiss in contempt at them, because they would recognise that the LORD had judged and humiliated them for their sins. When they were taken captive by their enemies, probably here thought of primarily as the later Babylonian invaders, the surrounding Gentile nations would ridicule them as the professed, but failing, people of God. They would suffer deep reproach for their sad condition. Even today we Christians open ourselves to the ridicule of unbelievers when we sin wilfully and suffer its consequences.

Finally, let us consider the very harmful effect that following ungodly legislation and wicked moral and spiritual practices can have on any nation, and especially one that has previously followed the laws of God as laid down in Scripture. Many Western nations and governments who used to order their lives very largely by the principles of Scripture and the gospel have, during the past half century, turned away from them and legislated laws and approved practices which the Word of God forbids at our peril. Gross immorality and judicial murder are enshrined in our official statute books. There is now no fear of God in our lands, and therefore we are beginning to suffer the fearful and disastrous consequences of so doing in our present broken and immoral societies. Most once strong nations decline in this way. Be warned, dear reader, and repent, before it is too late, and complete disaster overtakes us, as it did the two kingdoms of ancient Israel! What was proved true of them has been proved true of every other nation before and since, for we all share the same sinful nature as had they. God's universe is a moral universe, and there are inevitable and very painful consequences of offending against His moral and spiritual laws.

Micah Chapter 7

1. Micah, voicing the despair of the small godly remnant in Judah, laments the almost total godlessness of his nation and contemporary society, where murder and bribery were rife, and mutual trust had completely broken down, so that judgement was sure to overtake them, vv. 1-6.

While chapter 6 ended with an indictment of God's people Israel and a prediction of certain judgement that was imminent, at the beginning of chapter 7 Micah, representing the small nucleus of godly believers in the nation, voices their poignant confession of sin, and laments the total corruption around them. Calling down woe upon himself, Micah says that his nation is like an orchard after the harvest of summer fruits, or a vineyard after the gathering of the grapes. There is nothing to eat from it, and certainly not a first-ripe fig, which was considered an especial delicacy. Verse 2 explains what he means. He says that there are no good men, or righteous men, left in Israel; so godless have the LORD's professing earthly people become. In fact, there is murder on every hand, and everyone among them seems intent on destroying their fellow-brethren.

Micah now turns to describe the wickedness of the rulers and judges. They are intent on doing evil earnestly and diligently with both hands, that is, using all means in their power, and are successful in doing so. The rulers ask for the judges to condemn an innocent man, while the judges agree to comply, but require a bribe before acting. The influential man expresses his wicked desire, and the two of them conspire to achieve it in court. In this way poor Naboth was unjustly condemned to death on the orders of Ahab during the ninth century BC, see 1 Kings 21 verses 11-13. The best of men in the nation were as dangerously prickly to deal with as a brier, and the most upright of the leaders were just like a thorn hedge in their violent temperament and wicked dealings with their subordinates. The corruption was so widespread that God's judgement must fall on them soon, just as His watchmen, the true prophets of the LORD like Micah and Isaiah, had been predicting. The day of visitation, in the form of the coming foreign invasions previously mentioned, was at hand, yet when it did arrive, the leaders would have no idea what to do, because they had refused to listen to the warnings that their true prophets had been giving them over many years now.

Then, in verses 5-6, Micah bemoans the fact that all normal relationships and mutual trust had broken down in Israel, so that no-one could confide in anyone else, not even in their own closest family circles. In fact, there was universal treachery, as people discovered that their close relatives were their chief enemies in daily life. The Lord Jesus quoted this verse in Luke chapter 12 verse 53, when He predicted the enmity that accepting the gospel would bring between family members during this present age. Many true Christians have proved the truth of His warning there; often our closest relatives are our chief persecutors and critics when we make a bold commitment to Christ. It has happened many times in Jewish or Muslim countries especially; our simple love for Christ seems to provoke great hatred among our unsaved loved ones, so that many such believers have suffered ostracism, excommunication, or martyrdom, for their faith in the Saviour. Thus it was a very sad scene that Micah brought to the LORD in his vicarious confession of the nation's sins. However, in the next verses we find his triumphant response of true faith in his God.

2. Micah expresses his confidence in the LORD's ultimate salvation of His people Israel, after they have suffered His chastisement for their sins, and in their future blessing and expansion in the Millennial Kingdom, vv. 7-13.

Now, like his fellow-prophet Habakkuk about a century later, Micah, still voicing the thoughts of his fellow-believers in Israel, expresses his absolute confidence in the LORD. His faith is tangible and infectious as he says that he will look to the LORD, and wait expectantly for His salvation, certain that He will hear his prayers for His people. His faith is triumphing over the surrounding tragedy that he has just described. We today must feel like him, as we see the evidence of departure from God in our society with all its disastrous consequences. However, seeing all this, like Micah we should be encouraged to say, 'Therefore', because there is nothing else we can do to remedy the situation ourselves, 'we will look to God in implicit faith, and wait for Him to resolve matters in His own time and way at the second coming of Christ'.

In verses 8-10, Micah addresses Israel's enemies, who were about to swoop down on them in severe judgement. Let them not rejoice against Israel, nor gloat over their coming fate, because Micah was confident that they would recover from their disaster; even when the nation was sitting in the darkness of the imminent exiles, the LORD would be a light of hope to the faithful in the nation like himself. Israel's fall would not be permanent. Confessing the sin of his nation, Micah states that he will bear patiently the punishment that the LORD is going to lay upon him, and wait for Him to plead the nation's case again, and then to execute justice for them. He knew from the prophetic Scriptures that had already been written that the LORD would eventually bring him and his nation out into the light of salvation and recovery from the exiles, so that he, with his fellow-believing Jews, would witness the accomplishment of the LORD's righteous ways with them. These verses probably look even beyond the immediate exiles into Assyria and Babylon to their later dispersion and eventual regathering in the end times, for almost the very next verses, 11-12, clearly predict Israel's blessing in the Millennial Kingdom of Christ. Verse 10 says that, when Israel's enemies see their recovery and return, probably in the end times as well as after the exile to Babylon, they will be ashamed that they had ever made the taunt against Israel, 'Where is the LORD thy God?', casting doubt on the LORD's ability to keep His covenant-people. Instead, the faithful remnant of Israel will then witness the destruction and humiliation of their enemies like mud trampled down in the streets.

Then, in verses 11-12, inspired by the Spirit of God, Micah predicted some of the features of Jerusalem in the coming kingdom of Christ. These verses are difficult to translate and understand clearly, but probably refer chiefly to a time still future to us today. The AV/KJV translates verse 11 thus: 'In the day that thy walls are to be built, in that day shall the decree be far removed'. Some commentators think that this refers to the removal of the enemy's tyrannical decrees and laws under which Israel has suffered so much. Others suggest that the decree is actually the boundary of the city, which will be extended to accommodate an increased population. However, the verse is acknowledged to be rather obscure in meaning. The *Jamieson, Fausset, and Brown Commentary* comments as follows on the verse: " 'Thy walls are to be built' – under Cyrus, after the seventy years' captivity; and again, hereafter, when the Jews shall be restored... 'shall the decree be far removed' – namely, thy tyrannical decree or rule of Babylon shall be put away from thee, the statutes that were not good". It adds, "The Hebrew is against Maurer's translation, 'the boundary of the city shall be far extended', so as to contain the people flocking into it from all the nations".

Feinberg points out that the word used for 'walls' here, *gader*, usually refers to the boundary walls of a vineyard, rather than to defensive city walls, which will not be needed for Jerusalem during the peaceful Millennial Kingdom. Other Scriptures indicate that millennial Jerusalem will have some kind of boundary walls with twelve gates, but they will not be needed for military defence, see especially Ezekiel chapter 48 and Isaiah chapter 26 verse 1. In the latter verse, the word used for 'walls', *homoth*, is different from the one used here, and does seem to refer to military defensive walls, in parallel with the word 'bulwarks'. However, Isaiah says that God will appoint 'salvation' as the defensive walls of Jerusalem, a spiritual and supernatural defence rather than a military one.

Verse 12 should probably be translated as follows: 'In that day', that is, the beginning of the Millennial Kingdom, 'shall they', that is, the Jewish captives returning from the dispersion, 'come unto thee', the city of Jerusalem, 'from Assyria and the cities of Egypt', literally, from the fortified north-eastern boundary of Egypt, 'and from Egypt even to the River', Euphrates, 'and from sea to sea', from the Mediterranean in the west to the Persian Gulf in the east, 'and from mountain to mountain', from Sinai in the south to Hermon in the north. There will be a worldwide return of the scattered Jewish population to the Promised Land. J.M. Flanigan compares Isaiah chapter 27 verse 13, which predicts the same movement back to Jerusalem in response to the blowing of 'the great trumpet', the summoning *shofar*.

Verse 13 can be understood in one of two ways, depending on how we interpret and translate the word *ha-arets* here, because it can mean either 'the land', that is, the land of Israel, or 'the earth', meaning the rest of the world, the Gentile nations. Commentators are divided on the question. Many tend to support the view that Micah is predicting that the earth will be desolate because of the wicked deeds of its Gentile inhabitants, which is a very possible interpretation in view of other Scriptures which foretell the coming Tribulation before Christ returns in glory to set up His kingdom on earth. However, perhaps the preferable view in the immediate context of this prophecy is that it refers to the Promised Land of Israel in the interim period between Micah's day and the fulfilment of the prophecy just given concerning the return of the Jewish dispersion at the beginning of the Millennial Kingdom. Both this book and other prophetic books warn the apostate nation of Israel that, until the end times, the land of Israel will be desolate because of the many sins of the Jewish people during the Old Testament period and later. Just previously, Micah has warned his wayward people of imminent judgement and exile as a punishment for their sins, and he may well be continuing to follow up this same theme in the closing sections of his book. He would then be saying that there would be much tragedy and suffering before the predicted final salvation and blessing are enjoyed by his people.

3. Micah now prays that the LORD will shepherd His people Israel tenderly, as in former times, leading them into fertile pastures, while the LORD promises to show them marvellous things, as in the days of the Exodus, with the result that the hostile Gentile nations will be ashamed of their opposition to Him, be humiliated before Him, and turn in fear to acknowledge Him because of Israel, vv 14-17.

Micah turns in prayer to the LORD to plead with Him that He would, in His abundant mercy and grace, shepherd His people

Israel tenderly and kindly, despite all their grievous sins, because they are still His cherished flock, who form His chosen inheritance among the nations of the world. Let Him support them with His gentle staff, and not always chastise them with His harsh rod of correction. Let Him enable them to graze in rich pastureland, such as the fruitful fields of Mount Carmel and the good cattle-rearing plains of Bashan and Gilead in Transjordan, as He did in former years. To this earnest and heartfelt prayer the LORD immediately replies by assuring His faithful prophet that He will perform marvellous, miraculous deeds for His beloved people Israel in the future, just as He did when they came out of Egypt at the Exodus. This answer should be enough to encourage Israel to realise that the LORD would one day again intervene to preserve and protect them. He had lost none of His ancient power, and would act to vindicate His glory on their behalf. When He did so, the hostile Gentile nations would be humiliated before Israel, become speechless, and even turn in repentance to fear the LORD God of Israel because of all that He would do for and through His chosen earthly people. The nations would be compelled to lick the dust like serpents, and crawl out of all their hiding-places like worms into the light of His presence.

4. Finally, Micah praises the LORD for His incomparable pardoning grace, which assures him that He will ultimately have compassion on His people Israel, forgive their sins, and fulfil all His unconditional covenant-promises to Abraham and all the patriarchs, vv. 18-20.

As Micah concludes his solemn book of prophecy, which contains both warnings of imminent judgement and promises of ultimate great blessing and glory for his people Israel, he meditates on the meaning of his own name, which is 'Who is like the LORD?' He makes another play on words, or pun, here, as he did in chapter 1 to good effect. Despite all the preceding threats to Israel and Judah concerning exile and disaster for their many serious sins, Micah exults in the truth that the LORD is incomparable in His pardoning mercy and grace, and will ultimately forgive His people for their sins against Him. He is sure that his God will not retain His anger forever, because he knows that He really delights, not in judging and punishing mankind, but in showing mercy towards them. God will one day in the future turn again towards His people in blessing, and have compassion on them. Micah is here speaking for the faithful remnant in Israel, because we know, from other Scriptures, that it will only ever be a believing remnant who will finally enjoy their people's covenant-blessings and salvation, see Romans chapter 11. All their sins and iniquities will be atoned for and cast into the depths of the deepest sea. Micah was not given to reveal here how this would become possible through the sacrifice of Christ at Calvary, as his contemporary prophet Isaiah was greatly privileged to reveal in his chapter 53, but he was undoubtedly himself living in the good of that one sacrifice for sins forever prospectively, as were all Old Testament saints.

In verse 20, Micah triumphantly states his assurance of faith that the LORD will fulfil all His unconditional promises made to Jacob's wayward and failing nation Israel from the time of His covenant with Abraham in the Book of Genesis, and to all the later patriarchs, including His servant David, to whom He promised an everlasting dynasty and kingdom. God is always faithful to His promises, even when we prove unfaithful to Him. As the apostle Paul said in Romans chapter 11 verse 29, 'the gifts and calling of God are without repentance'. Yes, the nation of Israel has an assured future and hope, in spite of all their sins and punishment in the exiles and dispersion! These verses confirm that truth. Praise God, He is always true to His word!

Thus a prophecy which began in deepest gloom because of Israel and Judah's serious sins of moral and social injustice, which merited severe punishments in the impending two exiles, ends on a very high note of triumphant faith in God and His promises of final salvation, glory, and blessing for Israel in their own Promised Land during the future Kingdom of Christ. Yet we need to remember that this will only ever be possible because of the vicarious sacrifice of Christ on Calvary, which enables God to forgive our sins justly as well as mercifully and faithfully, Romans chapter 3 verses 21-26. Truly, there is no-one like the LORD our God in any way! Praise His Name!

Conclusion

May these five searching messages from the Minor Prophets act as light beams from a divine lighthouse, guiding us away from the dangers of many sunken rocks around us and into the safety of our heavenly harbour!

Joel warns us to repent of mechanical formalism in our professed worship of God, and thus to avoid His intervention in our lives to chastise us. If we do this, He will restore to us the wasted years of barrenness in our witness to Him, and pour out the blessings of His Spirit into our lives again, as He will in the world generally one day.

Amos warns us sternly to repent of all forms of social injustice and religious hypocrisy in our daily lives, and thus to be prepared to meet Him with a good conscience, because we love our neighbours as ourselves, as the law of God commands us to do. The alternative is disastrous judgement. Let us not refuse to listen to faithful preachers of God's word, just because they are from humble backgrounds, since they are often our best real friends.

Obadiah warns us to repent of the serious sins of natural pride in ourselves, Satan's original sin, and of Anti-Semitism, which is so prevalent in many parts of our world today. Let us realise that they are both foolish and will lead us into final judgement and disillusionment. God's chosen earthly people, Israel, will be vindicated one day, and all their opponents will be defeated. Let us put to death the deeds of the old nature.

Jonah warns us, when He calls us to serve Him in preaching

Conclusion

to the worst of sinners, to repent of our self-righteousness and disobedience to God's word just because they may have ill-treated us in the past. Let us realise that God loves all men regardless of race or behaviour, and wants them to be saved just as we have been. Let us also learn the lesson that success in preaching does not necessarily indicate the godliness of the preacher, but just proves the power of God's word to transform men's lives. Consider that Jonah's outlook was probably changed by God's dealings with him here, and so can ours be.

Micah warns us, as severely as does Amos, concerning the coming judgements for oppressing the poor and innocent while still professing to worship God; but he also encourages us to consider that, through Christ, the world and His people Israel will one day in the future be changed forever in the fulfilment of His unconditional promises to the patriarchs. Let us realise that God is incomparable both in His strict justice and in His sovereign mercy and the forgiveness of our sins, if we repent of them.

Therefore, let us follow these warning light beams into the safety of the heavenly harbour, and thus receive a full reward for our lives of witness and service for God. Yes, the searching messages of these so-called 'Minor Prophets' are still very relevant to us today in the twenty-first century AD, and should be heeded. May we, therefore, receive with meek humility God's implanted word!

Other Titles available by:
Malcolm C Davis

God's Weeping Prophet and Wayward People

This book considers Jeremiah's Prophecy and the Book of Lamentations. The pattern adopted by the author begins with an introduction, followed by a Concise Commentary, then concludes with Practical Studies in Major Themes and Recurring Phrases. This book is for those who cannot digest a very long and detailed commentary, but who value a succinct and readable analysis of all the chapters.

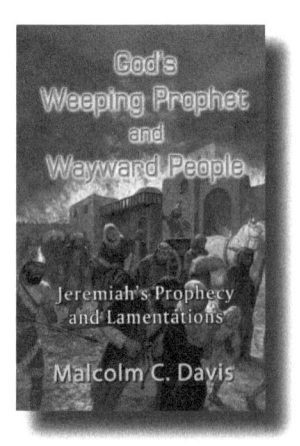

9781910513507

Living with the Glory of the Lord

Malcolm Davis commences by providing the reader with a "Concise Commentary on every chapter" of Ezekiel's Prophecy. The leading themes are identified in uncomplicated language and difficult passages and issues are clearly addressed.

The *Glory of the Lord* is found as a recurring theme throughout the entire prophecy. The reader is reminded that God is "glorious in holiness, fearful in praises, doing wonders".

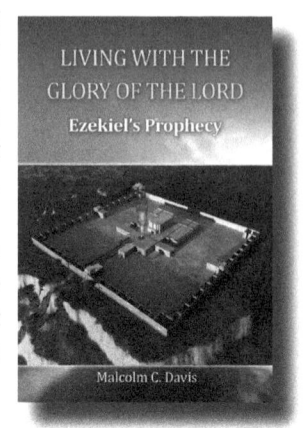

9781909803787

Anticipating the End Times

This book is a concise and readable commentary on the Old Testament Book of Daniel. He lived in momentous times of world empires, and also prophesied a great deal about the end times of world history. There are many current indications that we today are approaching the end times of which he wrote. This means that the Book of Daniel is very relevant to us, and therefore we need to understand its contents and message urgently.

9781907731020

When the Lord Remembers His Own

Zechariah's prophetic ministry ended two and a half millennia ago, but his Prophecy remains relevant today. As is noted in his other works, Malcolm Davis states, "This commentary has been written from a conservative Pre-millennial, Pre-tribulational standpoint, which accepts inspired Scripture at face value and believes that it should be interpreted as literally as is reasonable". His robust defence of the unity of Zechariah's prophecy is necessary and should be carefully considered by the reader. The prophecy presents the glories of Jehovah's Servant, the Branch, the Stone and the King riding on the foal of an ass.

9781910513057

The Saviour God and His Servant King

This book aims to help the reader to gain an overall grasp of this challenging prophecy, and especially to appreciate more deeply our unique Saviour God and His Servant King, Jesus Christ.

9781907731839

Israel's Broken-Hearted Prophet

Hosea's Prophecy is unique in Scripture, because it records how the Lord called one of His prophets to marry a woman whom He knew would prove to be unfaithful. The unhappy relationship which resulted was intended to illustrate very poignantly the Lord's tragic relationship with His unfaithful people Israel.

9781910513736